Six Thousand Signatures

My Trek Through Illinois Politics

Kathleen Smith Thomas

Laura Oleen Gough

ISBN

978-0-557-49889-5

To Dwight and Jeff

Thank you for your total and unconditional support!

We shall nobly save or meanly lose the last best hope of earth.

Abraham Lincoln, State of the Union Address, December 1, 1862

We are indeed, and we are today, the last best hope of man on earth.

Ronald Reagan, First Conservative Political Action Conference, January 25, 1974

Power corrupts, and absolute power corrupts absolutely.

Lord Acton of England

Introduction

One of the distinctive features of a Republic is the opportunity given to women and men to serve in elected office. Every elected official, from school board member to the President of the United States, plays a vital role in shaping the policies and direction our communities, our states, and ultimately our country will take. It is up to us, the electorate, to make sure we are represented well.

Of all the candidates running for the United States Senate in the 2010 Illinois Primary election, I was the one with the least political experience. Politics in general and campaigning in particular, as you will read in the following pages, is not for the faint-hearted. It can be overwhelming, frustrating and stressful; nevertheless, the opportunity is available for each of us. By running for office, I, along with my campaign manager, Laura Gough, hoped to take the mystique out of politics by showing that a "common citizen" can do this. Joe Biden (I use him because he was the catalyst for my running) represents the mind set of politicians who have been in office for extensive periods of time, and he reflects what is wrong with our current political situation. Anyone who has been inside the beltway for more than a couple of terms, unless the person is truly a saint, becomes part of the system itself. These politicians morph into part of the problem, rather than the solution. They feel that if they are not "bringing home the bacon" to their district or introducing new legislation, they cannot get re-elected, and that, above all else, becomes the mantra of politicians.

Every office deserves people who are grounded in the divinely ordained principles of life, liberty and the pursuit of happiness as guaranteed us in the Constitution. We need elected officials who are people of integrity and honesty…people who are incorruptible and willing to stand by the Constitution. We need people with maturity and common sense, people who know how to prevent liberty from becoming license. *We need citizen legislators—people who perform their civic duty and then return to their professions.*

Shortly after the Primary election in February 2010, a Republican meeting was held in Litchfield, a small town south of Springfield. Two single men, ages 27 and 28, one a U. S. Congressman and the other a Lt. Governor nominee, were introduced as "the new faces of the Republican party." Now, I do not doubt that these men intend to be honorable and honest. But an individual that young, with little to no life experience and with no family responsibilities, lacks the perspective of the everyday person that is essential to making public decisions. While civic service is praiseworthy, *making politics a career has proven detrimental to the health of our nation*—the temptation to become caught up in politics-as-usual may be overwhelming. This is not a statement about these particular young men; it is a comment about the nature of humans. Already the Congressman had proven himself a true Party man by endorsing, in the primary, the liberal Republican candidate for the Senate, Mark Kirk. Even though the Congressman disagreed with Kirk's vote on Cap and Trade and his stand on the Second Amendment, he still endorsed him. I can only assume it was for the sake of the Party, and in many politicians' minds, Party trumps principle. If we continue to accept this philosophy of Party above all else, we will continue to settle for mediocrity in our elected officials.

Laura and I have attempted to share in this book the story of our political journey in hopes that it will inspire and inform voters. Although we have chosen to tell it in Kathleen's voice, it is very much the story of both of us, two politically inexperienced women who wanted to make a difference in Illinois and the country. It was as much a voyage of personal growth for both of us as it was a duty that we felt must be done. In telling our story we relied upon notes, emails and detailed journal entries.

Our purpose here is not to denigrate individuals, but to expose some of the inner workings of campaigning and the election process. We wish to show the electorate what goes on behind the scenes—and to especially emphasize that the average citizen is just as smart, and often a lot smarter, than our politicians. In fact, it is essential that we embrace the democratic process in order for us to "nobly save, or meanly lose, the last best hope of earth."

Consider these questions as you read this book:

Is it possible for one lone citizen, devoid of party connections and no means of wealth, to be seriously considered for elected office?

Has the Republican Party become so focused on itself and the election process that it has lost sight of its vision for the country?

What is my list of criteria for a candidate?

Finally, in being a means to an end and not an end in itself, how do we reclaim the Republican Party?

Why I Ran

How do the people feel about T.A.R.P.?

For a couple of years I had privately entertained the thought of running for the United States Senate. I had become increasingly disillusioned and frustrated with the way Congress was treating the American people and the direction legislation was headed. I knew I was smart and capable enough to do as good a job as, if not better than, most of the legislators in office. But it was Joe Biden who made up my mind. I was watching him being interviewed in early spring 2009 when a reporter asked the Vice President, "How do the people feel about T.A.R.P.?" Biden flippantly answered, to the effect, "Oh, the people don't even know what T.A.R.P. stands for." I leapt out of my chair and, jabbing my finger toward the figure on the screen, yelled, "Troubled Asset Relief Program!" I was fuming. Biden had worked inside the beltway for over 36 years and had grown to think that *we the people* were ignorant and unaware of what transpires in Washington. This was the last straw for me and all the fuel I needed to begin actively participating in the Illinois Senate race.

It was Biden again who later reaffirmed my decision to run as he spoke at Senator Edward Kennedy's memorial service that summer. I had already begun circulating a petition to get my name on the February Primary ballot when I heard him relate this story:

John, I remember we were talking about Angola once. And you and Teddy were working out a deal with some of our more conservative friends. And you agreed on a particular course of action. And I was, along with your colleague Dick Clark -- you and Dick and Teddy and myself, in Teddy's office. And being naive as I was as a young senator, we started about how we were going to approach this issue on the floor. And Teddy said, we've got to do this. And I said but -- I said, but that's not what we said. We told these guys we were going to do that.

And Teddy very politely tried to say to me, well, no, we're going to -- this went on for a few minutes. And finally, John, in a roaring voice said, "Biden, what the hell do you think this is? Boys State?" That was my introduction to the squeeze of Kennedy and Culver. What the hell do you think this is? Boys State?

-Joe Biden, August 28, 2009, Kennedy Memorial Service

A few polite laughs from the audience followed, but I was stunned. Had it become so acceptable to lie and deceive in the Halls of Congress that the Vice President felt it was okay to openly admit to it? Were integrity and honesty merely words to joke about? I know there are plenty of backroom deals, pats on the back, and winks and nods on Capitol Hill; I am not naïve. But in sharing that story, the Vice President was also sending this message—*If you stay in Washington long enough, expect to become corrupted.*

So, it followed nicely when Bernard Schoenburg (political reporter, Springfield State Journal-Register) asked me why I was running and I replied, "Because I'm tired of yelling at my TV." Apparently, my response resonated with a lot of people. Across the state, frustration over the disconnect between citizens and elected officials was growing among both Republicans and Democrats. Illinoisans living south of I-80 and away from Chicago's urban culture were the angriest—they were not being fairly represented and hadn't been for decades. The vast majority of politicians representing and governing the state came from Chicago—the central and southern parts of the state have always had to scratch and fight for representation of their interests and, all too often, the fight is lost to the interests of Chicago and corrupt politics. At political events I would say, "Illinois is a beautiful state, the heartland of America, the breadbasket of the world. It is the home of Abraham Lincoln and Ronald Reagan. But what are we known for?" I would then answer, "Political corruption." In the media and in conversation across the country "Chicago" represents all that is wrong in American politics. I discovered that people were elated to have a candidate from anywhere other than Chicago and someone not tied to corrupt Illinois state politics. I was happy to offer myself as something different.

Studied diligently all day on the Cap and Trade issue and global warming. My brain is fried...went to walk the dog and had several phone calls when I returned.

Journal Entry-September 7

The frustration felt by me and many Illinoisans reached beyond the feeling that America's governing body is arrogant and ignorant; it was a frustration that the ideas we disdained during the Cold War were taking root on our own soil. Ronald Reagan said that, "The ultimate determinant in the struggle now going on for the world will not be bombs and rockets but a test of wills and ideas—a trial of spiritual resolve: the values we hold, the beliefs we cherish and the ideals to which we are dedicated." Many Americans are feeling that now is a time when the values, beliefs and ideals of which Reagan spoke are being threatened by a liberal ideology.

I grew up in a time when Americans treasured freedom and feared socialism. Our teachers and parents preached the importance of hard work, making our own way, and offering a charitable hand to our neighbors. But in 2008 we elected a president whose thinking is contrary to that—whose statist ideas threaten to take away many of our freedoms. Since taking office, he and like-minded individuals have pushed the creation of a nanny state where the government decides what we will eat, the cars we will drive, what our children will learn, and the health care we will receive. I believe that safety nets are important, and programs are needed to help those that cannot help themselves, but these safety nets need to be operated on a local and state level, not the federal level. I sincerely wanted to be on the front lines in the battle against this big government ideology. I wanted to take my resolve to Washington.

During the summer of '09, I downloaded and read the eleven hundred page health care bill that was up for vote in the House of Representatives. I thought that since I was going to run for the Senate I should know the specifics of the legislation. So I plunged in and started reading. About five hundred pages into it I was ready to give up, go to a movie and eat five pounds of chocolate. I could not believe how convoluted and disingenuous the bill was. Still, I persevered and finished. I met several people during the beginning of the healthcare debate who also took it upon themselves to become informed by reading the original bill—something most Senators and Congressmen had not done. Congressman John Conyers of Michigan dumbfounded us all when he said at a National Press Club Luncheon, "What good is reading the bill if it's a thousand pages…" Of course, the version of the bill I was reading became obsolete rather rapidly as it evolved and changed so many times that it was a chore to keep on top of it by myself. I never finished reading the over two thousand page Senate version.

I also tackled the Cap and Trade bill. This bill was extra controversial in this particular Senate race as the leading Republican contender, Mark Kirk, voted for it in the House of Representatives. It passed the House and was sitting in the Senate in Washington during the entire campaign. The concept of the bill seemed like a good idea—the government would charge large companies to clean up their pollution and give us clean air. On first perusal my initial reaction to the bill was, "It certainly looks as if there is a lot of room for graft and corruption."

Continuing my study of the Cap and Trade Bill, I read the Intergovernmental Panel on Climate Change (IPCC) reports from the United Nations. These were the reports legislators and global warming promoter Al Gore used to shore up his argument for global warming. This was tedious reading as I am not a scientist, but I trudged along and was able to understand the gist of it. One paragraph in particular caught my eye and I called an energy developer/consultant that I know. I said, "Do I understand this correctly? It sounds as if the sea *might* rise several inches in two hundred years and the temperature *might* rise several degrees in one hundred years. That hardly sounds like a crisis to me." He said yes, I understood correctly. "Then why," I asked, "does the media spout that there is a big global warming crisis? And Al Gore gets millions of dollars from people buying carbon credits?" It was an eye-opener to me to learn that most people, especially political aids and journalists, just read the executive summaries. In this case, those executive or policy summaries were written by someone who, metaphorically speaking, was 'in bed' with Al Gore.

I continued to study Senate testimony and other writings and came to the conclusion that Cap and Trade was a bad bill. Besides not being capable of cleaning the air as it purported, it would end up, I believe, to be a tax of astronomical proportion. Throughout the campaign I drew attention to the fact that front running candidate Mark Kirk voted in the House for this nonsensical and punitive bill—legislation that we will be paying for in higher prices on everything from our clothes and food to our homes and cars. Without exception, the people I spoke to were upset about Cap and Trade and Mark Kirk's Yes vote.

The point I want to make here is that the job of studying legislation and determining its value is not rocket science. The fact is, most clear-thinking intelligent citizens are capable of the job. The Senate is the deliberative body of Congress and, as I see it, our Senators should be intimately familiar with proposed legislation. But our legislators are failing to do this; they are introducing legislation that is too long and complicated. They are failing to read and understand the far reaches of the bills that are introduced and therefore, they are failing to make good common sense decisions. James Madison, the Father of the

Constitution, stated this idea best in the Federalist papers. He wrote, "It will be of little avail to the people that the laws are made by men of their own choice if the laws be so voluminous that they cannot be read, or so incoherent that they cannot be understood; if they be repealed or revised before they are promulgated, or undergo such incessant changes that no man who knows what the law is today, can guess what it will be tomorrow." Today we are seeing a Congress whose Yes or No votes and the legislation they introduce are too often based on re-election strategies. This is why Kirk voted the way he did for Cap and Trade and why he has to back-peddle to explain his vote during his run for the Senate.

We have strayed from the simple philosophy of representation that the Founding Fathers established. During our country's infancy Senators and Congressmen were elected by the people, served one or two terms, and then returned home to their farms, stores, or legal practices, etc. Abraham Lincoln is a prime example of this when he served in the U. S. House of Representatives. Because we keep re-electing our representatives over and over again they become far removed from us. While in office they also establish monetary connections and are able to accrue millions of dollars for their next election. They become professional politicians who too often take on a larger-than-life persona. They cease to be servants of the people and become celebrities and/or politicians in the most pejorative sense of the word. They don't have time to read the legislation because they are spending their time fund raising and making plans for re-election.

I love America. On Veterans' Day I went to Camp Butler National Cemetery to pay tribute to our war veterans. Laura Gough's father, who served in W.W. II, is buried there. When we arrived, a group of cameramen were setting up to film the ceremony. Laura asked, "Do you want to stand over there in front of those cameras?" I said, "No, it seems kind of scummy to take advantage like that." I just enjoyed being there and looking at all of the old people and noticing the ones my age were Vietnam Veterans. I thought of my eighty-nine year old Dad and his service to his country in World War II and Korea. I thought about my son and his service in the Iraqi War and Guantanamo Bay. Visiting a National Cemetery is always emotionally overwhelming. You walk past row after row after row of the headstones of men and women who served to protect and defend our rights and our freedoms. It was especially poignant to me at that time as I considered how those liberties are being eroded and how, if America doesn't wake up, we will lose all that has been fought for these past couple hundred years.

Journal Entry—November 11

Six Thousand Signatures

I'm not delusional.

In August 2009 I hosted a dinner party in my home. The casual gathering had been planned weeks before my decision to run for the Senate and about twenty-five friends from my church were there. I chose to use this setting to announce that I was running for the United States Senate. Everyone was thrilled with the announcement and enthusiastically agreed to collect signatures for my petition. Five thousand signatures of registered Illinois voters were required to get my name on the primary ballot. My goal, however, was six thousand because I had been told it was likely that my petition would be challenged and signatures thrown out. I designated October twenty-fifth as the deadline to have each notarized page of ten signatures (six hundred pages) back in my hands. I planned to file with the State Board of Elections on the twenty-sixth.

Laura thought I was joking when I asked her to be my campaign manager that night. Her past campaigning experience consisted of placing yard signs in front of her house and attending a couple of rallies for presidential hopefuls. But before the last guest left the dinner party she had agreed to the task with the stipulation, "Until you find a real campaign manager." Like me, she was aggravated by the state of affairs in Washington and was excited about getting politically involved. Her greatest strength, she said, was that she doesn't like to lose.

The previous day while at Republican Headquarters, I learned that candidates could collect signatures at the Republican tent at the Illinois State Fair in Springfield which was set to open the next day. Laura's twenty-year-old daughter Lindsay, was coaxed into taking the first shift at the Fair. I gave her a full-page position paper I had typed up and copied by the hundreds and asked her to give them to people when they signed the petition. We were pleased with her report that she had gotten forty-two signatures during the two hours she was there. Disheartening, however, was her description of the inside of the tent. To our surprise, and at the beginning of our rapid learning curve, campaigning was well under way—banners hung on the inside walls of the tent and tables were set up with stacks of sleek-looking literature. A few of the candidates in various races were giving out embossed trinkets like pens and pencils. Eric Wallace was offering free copies of the book he authored and Randy White's nail files were very popular. We felt we were behind in the game…way behind.

Apparently, people visiting the State Fair want refrigerator magnets and chip clips and don't want to be bothered with reading a lengthy description of a candidate's political philosophy. A few of us sat down at my computer to design a flyer. By eleven o'clock that night we were fairly happy with

I'm not delusional. But what am I supposed to do? Sit on my butt at home and do nothing? I am doing more than marching and protesting…I am offering myself as an alternative choice. I am offering myself so people can truly do something different…they can vote something different.

Journal Entry-October 26

the single sided, one-third page bullet point handout that briefly explained who I was. Laura worked on it some more during the night and at eight a.m. we headed out to find a copy machine. Two copy service centers and two hours later, I had a stack of six hundred red card stock flyers in my hand and I headed for the State Fair. During the next ten days we made several trips to Office Depot to replenish our supply. Over the two weeks at the State Fairs in Springfield and DuQuoin, and with six volunteers working a total of near one hundred hours, we gave away five thousand flyers and collected four thousand, five hundred signatures.

Collecting signatures consumed my life for the next two months. Although I still needed to concern myself with research, fundraising and getting my name known, I was keenly aware that the campaign would come to an abrupt end if I did not have the signatures I needed by the end of October. I asked everyone I knew to commit to getting signatures. I gave them suggestions of good places to get the signatures and I continued to remind and encourage everyone with frequent emails.

The election process varies from state to state with each state having its own set of requirements for getting a name on its election ballot. Many states have caucuses or pre-primary conventions. Some states base their signature requirement on a percentage; others require a potential candidate to file through their county or state Party Chair. In some states there is a filing fee. In Illinois, candidates running for Federal office need five thousand signatures to be on the Primary ballot. A candidate wanting to run as an Independent in the General Election needs a minimum of twenty-five thousand signatures. Although the signatures requirement seemed high to many of us collecting them, the process in our state is comparatively simple.

Ten days before the first day of filing we were just above the 5,000 minimum signatures. David Bridges, a tireless signature gatherer and supporter, had been hitting it hard for a few weeks and was as worried as I was about meeting the required number. During that final week we contacted everyone we knew who had a petition and begged them to get it notarized and returned right away. We challenged all of my supporters to get another thousand signatures by the 25th. Another volunteer, Miriam Fleshman, took

> *Didn't sleep that well, and woke up before the alarm. Why am I so nervous about filing? I don't have to say or do anything...just present my petitions.*
>
> *Journal Entry-Oct. 26*

the challenge seriously and chased people down in the Meijer grocery store parking lot one afternoon. She got six signatures before someone complained to management and she was asked to leave the premises. Every single signature was needed. Petitions that were in various parts of the state came trickling in and then on October 25th I made the final count—6040 signatures!

I took the 600 plus page petition to Fedex Kinkos that Saturday night to have two holes drilled in the top of the stack of papers. A few more petitions were handed to me on Sunday night which I added to the pile. I filled out the required paperwork, bound the whole thing together at the top with the two long screws and nuts I had bought at Lowes for that purpose, and, since it was a requirement, I numbered pages late into the night.

It poured buckets that night. We had heard from several sources that, traditionally, some people spend all night on the steps of the State Board of Elections on the eve of filing in order to be at the head of the line; we thought we ought to do that. Laura's son, Curtis volunteered to spend the night outside and two of my earliest supporters, Sherryl and Jerry Clark, parked their R.V. in front of the building with my name emblazoned across the side of it. At around nine o'clock in the evening, a television reporter, curious about the "Kathleen Thomas" sign and the few sidewalk campers, stopped and interviewed Curtis. The next day he was on channel 20 News wearing a "Kathleen Thomas for U.S. Senate" t-shirt and with my banner perfectly placed behind his right shoulder. The rain began some time after midnight, but undaunted, Curtis held our place with only a lawn chair to sleep in and an umbrella to keep him dry.

Went to husband's barber, Mike...while in the shop a Precinct committeeman came in with petitions for signatures. Mike introduced me to him and said I too was collecting signatures and would he take one of my sheets around. He said he was gathering signatures for Andy McKenna, who had just thrown his hat in the ring for the Governor's race...then added..."I am sick of these prima donna politicians...we do all the work for them."

Journal Entry--Oct 16

Laura relieved him at 5:30 a.m. so that he could go home to change out of his wet clothes and get to work by seven.

I arrived a little after seven o'clock and got in line with the growing crowd. I looked around and noted that there was easily one woman to every twenty-five men. I am a short woman and felt swallowed up in a sea of male politicians. Men walked up, gathered and smacked each other on the back and everyone seemed to know everyone else, except me. If there was a good old boy network, this was it, and this is what it felt like to be excluded. That night I reflected in my journal that "maybe if I were a tall woman I would get more attention." I did my best to be visible and a couple of reporters asked me a few questions before the doors opened at eight o'clock. Laura went in with me where my petition was first looked at by a woman who then told us to follow the yellow arrows which took us down the hall, up the stairs, down another hall, up more stairs and then to a table where a gentleman typed my information into a computer. He handed me a receipt to proof and sign and I was filed! It all took about seven minutes. Laura and I walked out the front doors of the building and were very grateful we did not have to stand in the line that wrapped around the block. A total of 886 candidates filed that day.

Candidates and their aides did not *choose* to stand in that long line in the wee hours of the morning because they were anxious to turn in their petitions—we had, after all, seven days to file with the State Board of Elections. The draw to file on that morning had to do with the order that the candidates' names would appear on the ballot. It worked like this—every petition that was in line when the officials came outside to mark the end of the line at eight A.M. were counted as filed at eight o'clock. Those names would be entered in the future lottery-style drawing that determined the order of names. There is some thought that the first name on the ballot has a two to five percent advantage on Election Day. Some people believe there are similar benefits to having your name last on the ballot. Patrick Hughes filed his petition after October 26th, withdrew it until every other Senate candidate filed, and a few hours later filed again, guaranteeing him the last spot on the ballot.

The drawing was held in November on a day I was driving north to Chicago. Laura went to the State Board of Elections so we could find out first hand where my name would end up. Like a lottery drawing, numbered ping pong balls which corresponded with the name of each candidate alphabetically were placed in a wooden box then drawn out one at a time. About twenty people, election officials, reporters and cameramen, and a few aides representing various campaigns were in the exact room where I had begun the filing process. Several cameras recorded the event. The Senate race was the second drawing, so within five minutes we knew the order the names would be on the ballot—Lowery, Kirk, Martin, Thomas, Arrington, Hughes. I could not have had a worse spot!

The Players

Do you want to see a Reagan Conservative take the Senate seat?

At the Palatine Township Republican endorsement session I attended I was asked what I thought about President Obama's announcement the previous day where he discussed America's strategy for Afghanistan. The President said he would send 40,000 troops and then he gave the timetable for withdrawal. My response to the question was, "Well, my husband, Dwight, was a football coach for many years and one thing I know is that you don't give the playbook to the enemy." There was standing applause and a few cheers to my answer.

Maybe it is Dwight's career in football that makes me compare so much in life to a game. Campaigning truly was a competitive game that involved strategy, teamwork, perseverance and knowing the opposition. During the six months I spent on the campaign trail I got to know my opposition, the other candidates. We saw and spoke to each other at events, Laura and I studied their websites and read their press releases, and I had occasional phone conversations with some of them. What follows in this chapter is a description of the players as I saw them in this particular political game.

In the beginning there were nine Republican U.S. Senate candidates scrambling for signatures. There was a spectrum of political ideology among the nine of us, representing the very liberal to the very conservative. This is not a new phenomenon as races usually have a variety of candidates. Both Republican and Democrat parties include people with a wide range of political beliefs. Both parties also have the ever unpopular moderates, who are often seen as fence-sitters. The current political atmosphere is indicative of the desire of many people, Republicans and Democrats, who want to return to the basic tenets of government, which are outlined in the Constitution. I have always been conservative and during the campaign I emphasized the current administration's blatant disregard for the Constitution.

John Arrington was the first candidate I met. I had seen his literature displayed on a table in the Republican tent at the State Fair and I learned that he had his own tent set up near the main entrance of the fair, but it wasn't until the end of the first week that he came into the Republican tent and we introduced ourselves. One day he brought his wife and children with him and they seemed like a nice family. I really didn't know what to think about John. My first impression was that he was too slick to be a 'citizen legislator' and for some reason I thought he was favored by the Party. Later he mentioned to me that the Party did not want him to run, which then made me think that he was a threat to their preferred candidate. At this point in the campaign I did not even know the names of all the players and, lacking political savvy, I assumed John was a front runner.

OK, David said, why in the world did I go from school board to the senate! And I said...why not? And then blah, blah, blah,...common sense, intelligence, any citizen can do this that has those attributes, take mystique out of politics...anyone inside the beltway can't help but be influenced by the power, special interests, and they lose touch with reality....talked about how I studied cap and trade....more blah blah...said I wasn't naive or sophomoric, more blah, blah, blah.

When he mentioned about PH distinguishing himself as a Reagan Conservative...I said, I know...bless his heart...
He seemed to be asking me how I was different from the judge or Arrington.
He said at the end...on the outside chance you didn't win... (I interjected, oh you're sweet)...he laughed...would I be politically active and run again...I said I would stay involved in politics but more from educating the voters...it is so different what goes on behind the scenes and what is put out front...but I probably wouldn't run again. Anyway, all in all, nice interview

January 7, 2010 email from Kathy to Laura about a phone interview with David Kidwell from the Chicago Tribune

Over the next few months I got to know John better and I realized he was not a slick politician, but very much a "regular" person who was a really nice guy and who was almost always late to events. I especially liked his wife. John was politically conservative; however, he did not appear to have a good grasp on the issues. Often when he was asked something he was unsure how to answer, he would resort to his story about "the yellow bus". It was a narrative about how years ago his father had seen the need for a better transportation choice in their community, so he painted the family car yellow and began a bus service which eventually included actual busses. When John or his siblings wanted a job, his dad would tell them to "go and make one"! He was honest and sincere in the telling of the yellow bus story and it spoke much to his character. The most effective and confident I ever saw John was when he spoke to a group of youth at an inner city magnet school. They liked John and he was relaxed and articulate in front of them. It struck me that he would be an excellent motivational speaker for young people.

One non-Senate candidate was in the tent at the fair all day every day. Randy White, who was running for Lieutenant Governor, told me up front that I seemed nice but he was voting for John. John was his man. During these first days of campaigning I felt alone and small and kept asking myself "What in the world am I doing here?" and "I don't have the political expertise to do this" and "How can I do this? I don't know anyone and I have no political connections." But I kept plugging along and every so often someone would say something like, "I wish I had the courage to do what you're doing" or "thank you for doing this" and, frequently, "I am so glad to see a woman in this race". Comments like this would energize me and keep me going one more day.

At times it was difficult being in the tent with Randy and John because they, along with a young blonde buxom girl working for gubernatorial candidate Kirk Dillard, so dominated the space. I was strong in the sense that I could not be bribed, bought, or have my mind changed about my principles, but I was not yet brazen in asking people to sign and would quietly approach someone and give them my spiel—"Hi, my name is Kathleen Thomas and I'm running for the United States Senate. Would you please sign my petition?" Most people were happy to sign in order to allow someone who was different and not "in" with the Party to appear on the ballot.

Robert Zadek showed up at the very end of that first week. He was gregarious and eager to grab your ear to explain his tax proposal. Robert has had a very successful career as a businessman making millions of dollars. Although likable, he seemed to lack the public charisma that would draw people to support him. His fiancé, Rose, often travelled with him and I came to know her even better than Robert. She was delightful and genuine; I thought that maybe she should be running! Robert's petition was challenged and ultimately his name did not appear on the Primary ballot, but he continued to attend events as he planned to run as an Independent in the November election. If he is able to gather the twenty-five thousand signatures needed and can make it through the petition challenging process, he may be the only conservative Senate candidate on the ballot.

I travelled to the DuQuoin State Fair in Southern Illinois, where I met Don Lowery (or Judge, as most people called him) for the first time. Throughout the campaign he would contact me and ask if I was going to such and such an event and he filled me in on who he knew was going to be there. Apparently, he had connections (or "spies", as he referred to them) in Chicago because he was always in the know about the latest shenanigans of Martin, Hughes, Kirk or the Republican Party. Lowery would tell me, every time I saw him, "Stay in the race Kathy, we all need to stay in the race and beat Mark Kirk." He would also remind me that we were exercising our Constitutional right as citizens to run for the Senate. And while it is true that we had every right and reason to run in this race, the reality was that Mark Kirk would win unless the public woke up and became outraged over the fact that his voting record was liberal, both socially and fiscally. Although I knew that some Republicans wanted this kind of liberal, I felt that most voters were unaware of his record.

I noticed that later in the campaign, Lowery seemed to shift his focus from Kirk to Patrick Hughes. After the State Journal-Register's endorsement of Kirk, Don called me and not only sounded disappointed, but surprised that the editorial board did not press Hughes more about the fact that he hadn't voted in any public election until only a few years ago. I told Don, concerning Hughes' voting record, "Let it go." This time it was me telling the Judge to stay focused. "The one we need to go after is not Hughes, it is Kirk; he is the liberal, and he is the one we need to beat. Lay off Hughes and focus on Kirk."

During the late stages of the campaign I felt an urgency to inform the public about Mark Kirk's liberal voting record. Although many voters were aware that he was pro-choice on the abortion issue, most people I talked to did not know about his No vote to the banning of partial-birth abortions. Eight days before the election I spoke to a former city mayor who planned to vote for Kirk. After listening to me speak and after I explained Kirk's abhorrent partial-birth abortion vote, he took one of my yard signs and vowed to take down his Kirk sign.

I saw and shook hands with Patrick Hughes for the first time at the DuQuoin State Fair. I thought he did a good job speaking at DuQuoin; he seemed articulate and intelligent. There were several times during the campaign that I heard him speak from the heart. At the State Journal-Register endorsement session, I was greatly impressed with the way he passionately and vehemently confronted Mark Kirk on his No vote to ban partial-birth abortion. But most of the time he sounded scripted. Hughes constantly said he was the only one who could beat Mark Kirk. And although I didn't agree with him, I could live with that statement. But when he started saying he was the *only* conservative candidate running (as he did when he was on the radio with Mark Levin), I was irritated because that was just not true. After the Levin radio interview my sister, Becky, who had met Hughes at an earlier event, confronted him about the false statement. He came back by getting in her face, shaking his finger at her and saying, "I can say anything I want, anytime I want, to anyone I want to." As his aide pulled him away and down the stairs, Hughes looked back over his shoulder and yelled, "Why don't you go back to Texas?" Now, maybe he was having a bad day and maybe the stress was getting to him, but, no matter how you look at it, his behavior was inappropriate.

Next to Mark Kirk, Hughes easily spent the most money. He lost probably because he was not a good candidate and he relied heavily on anti-Kirk sentiment. Throughout the course of the campaign he seemed to offend as many people as he won over and the reputation of his highly-paid consultant was questionable.

Andy Martin, another candidate, and I later learned, a *perennial* candidate, went hard after Patrick Hughes and Mark Kirk. At one of the 9/12 forums, Hughes had, true to form, started his three minutes of introduction with the enthusiastic shout, "Who wants to see a real Reagan Conservative?" The crowd, of course, cheered and he went on to tell them why they should vote for him. Andy Martin got up and took the microphone right after Hughes was done and said, "I'm so glad he asked who the real Reagan conservative is…I appreciate the introduction, because that would be me!" Martin held the mike and went on a rant about sending Mexico the medical and educational bills the illegal Mexicans had incurred and he said, to the effect, "that will stop them from coming over! Once they get the bill, that will do it!" Months later Martin went after Kirk in his radio ads that hit the air around Christmas. The ads were sensationalist, calling Kirk a homosexual and a de facto pedophile. One of my staff members said, "I like it when Andy's there. I consider him the entertainment factor." I confess that I referred to Martin, affectionately, as Crazy Andy.

I formally met Andy Martin at DuQuoin. The first time I saw him, however, was a few weeks earlier at the meeting of the Republican County Chairmen. This was back when I thought the playing field was level and I had a good chance of becoming the Party's Senate candidate. Andy McKenna, at that time president of the Illinois Republican Party, stood at the podium conducting the meeting when he pointed to a large tall man at the back of the room and said, "You need to leave!" The man he was addressing responded, "This is a public meeting and I have the right to be here!" The exchange continued and the confrontation got nasty. I turned to the man next to me and asked, "Who is that?" He told me it was Andy Martin and that he had a lawsuit against the Illinois Republican Party…something about running or not being allowed to run—I was never clear on what it was all about. Later I learned that Andy was formerly known as Anthony Trigona and that he had been involved in politics on several levels for years…kind of a fixture who claimed to be a muckraker, exposing "secrets" on everyone from Obama to Mark Kirk.

As McKenna was wrapping up the Republican County Chairman's meeting he said that, "In view of the fact that I believe we need to hit the ground running in January, since the Primary is in February, I am stepping down now as president and allowing the new president, Pat Brady, to take the reins of the Illinois Republican Party. I know we will all get behind him and help him." And then McKenna proceeded to introduce the "new face" for the Republican Party who was running for the Senate…Mark Kirk! "Kirk is the man we need to support for the Senate." Did I hear him right!? *He had just announced to every Party Chair who they should support?!*…So much for the Party keeping an impartial stance in the Primary.

The first time I met Mark Kirk was at a function in Palatine. The first time he acknowledged me was several weeks later at the Southtown Star endorsement session. At the Springfield State Journal-Register endorsement session he displayed arrogance stereotypical of politicians. During the meeting, when the questioning turned to the Healthcare Bill, he leaned back in his chair, turned slightly to his aide and asked for a piece of paper. "Let me explain about the Healthcare bill," he said to all of us in the room. He proceeded to draw a chart to illustrate how a young man, for example, will pay a disproportionately high amount of money into the healthcare system if the Healthcare Bill were to pass. He drew lines and bars and talked…yadayadayada. He was proud of the fact that he was the author of a five hundred page Healthcare Bill. I sat there thinking…five hundred pages?! We don't want 500 pages…we don't want 1,000 or 2,000 pages…We don't want a healthcare bill at all. What we want are insurance and litigation reform!

Mark Kirk stayed above the fray. He was running a stealth campaign, keeping himself aloof and not standing up next to his opponents. He did not allow the public to get a side by side comparison of himself and the other candidates. In this way he also stayed above the issues by refusing to meet with the rest of the candidates for a debate. The Illinois Republican Party held a debate for the gubernatorial candidates, complete with theatrics; but they would not schedule one for the Senate candidates. And of course not, they had already chosen Kirk. Florida's Senate candidates Crist and Rubio not only got a debate, but also Chris Wallace as the moderator! But I digress.

Three other candidates were hoping to get their names on the Primary ballot. I met Bob Kuna at DuQuoin. Kuna filed with around five hundred signatures; he lost a challenge to his petition because he did not meet the five thousand signature requirement and, therefore, his name did not appear on the ballot. I never met Ed Varga, but his website was very entertaining, complete with a video of him playing the guitar and singing. I don't know how successful his signature gathering campaign went, but before the filing date he announced that he was dropping out because of personal reasons. Eric Wallace seemed to be a fairly strong candidate, but he too decided not to file and announced that he was considering running as an Independent.

In mid-November, Patrick Hughes called me and asked if I had talked with the Judge (Don Lowery) and I replied, "Yes, about a week ago." He said, "No, no, more recently. I spoke with Lowery yesterday and he is going to set up a meeting with you and John Arrington and him and me and we're going to discuss all of you dropping out and supporting me." He continued, saying that the other candidates had promised to drop out and support him if there was a front runner. He explained that he got into the race because Mark Kirk was an unacceptable candidate and whoever came out on top would be supported by the others. "I am encouraging and asking the other candidates to support my candidacy," he said. "I can beat Kirk and it would be worth your while to support me." He went on and on about how he had raised a bunch of money, was getting national coverage, and how the Wall Street Journal had interviewed him...Finally, I interrupted him by saying, "I can't believe Mark Kirk voted Yes for Cap and Trade. I'll talk with the Judge." He blathered on some more and then he said, "I'll see you tomorrow in Chicago."

I called Don Lowery right away and explained the phone call from Patrick. "Wait just a minute, Kathy, let me pull over and get my notes." I told him what Patrick had said and he replied, "I never said I would drop out. That is just wrong." Lowery went on to say that Patrick had told him that John Arrington and I were going nowhere with our campaigns and Hughes wondered what planet we lived on. He had said that he (Lowery) was a respected judge and was going to get his "butt kicked" and lose that respect. He said that Andy Martin was going to be arrested. "Patrick Hughes is an arrogant guy and I don't like him," Lowery said. I told him (Lowery) to set up the meeting if he wanted to and I would attend, but of course I would not agree to drop out. He wanted us (me, John Arrington, and himself) to "go into the meeting and say to Hughes that if he is so concerned about splitting the ticket then he needs to drop out and support one of us!"

Half way through the campaign, John Arrington, Don Lowery and I were all at a Republican endorsement session in Barrington, a suburb of Chicago. I was joking with them about what a perfect candidate we would be if we could roll ourselves into one—a Black, female, Ph.D. judge…now that would be an unbeatable candidate! Lowery and Arrington also told me the negative things Patrick Hughes' campaign had been writing about them and attempting to disseminate on the web and in some instances through snail mail. I mentioned that, since I hadn't been attacked, I was feeling left out.

Andy Martin had said that he wouldn't attend the endorsement sessions, but he did. He had mentioned to Don Lowery that all of the endorsement sessions were pre-determined in favor of Mark Kirk and we were just wasting our time. That was why I was surprised to see him at an endorsement session in Libertyville, another Chicago suburb. Martin and I were both waiting out in the small front office area of the Republican Headquarters at Libertyville and we could hear laughter coming from the back room. Patrick Hughes showed up and I told him that Kirk was still in the back room and at this point we were about 30 minutes behind schedule. I was up next and, quite frankly, after listening to all of that laughter, and knowing I was in Kirk's "backyard" I absolutely did not care about the outcome. I knew beyond any doubt that they would be endorsing Kirk. They were all talking as I entered the room and kept talking as I started speaking. Eventually they quieted down and some were kind enough to throw me a few questions. One man even commented on my campaign literature, singling out my "calling card". Afterward I saw on their website a message from the Chairman about their endorsement of Kirk. He also mentioned in it that Hughes was young and immature but good luck with his political career in the future and they threw a bone to Arrington. The article made no mention of me. I later learned that the person who wrote it was a friend of Hughes. I felt badly for Hughes at this point because it seemed he was expecting this particular endorsement.

Meeting and getting to know these different candidates under these unusual circumstances was an eye-opening experience. It was also interesting to meet candidates from the other races. Aside from the power, one of the enticements to seek a United States Congressional seat is the $172,000 salary. This figure does not include the perks and benefits of the job. Unless candidates' motives are a pure desire to be an honorable civil servant, the only real incentive is to get re-elected. The electorate will have to dig deep at every election to determine who the real person is behind the image.

I Never Vote for Women

She looks like a skeleton from a video game.
Well, a friendly one.

In the late fall I was inundated with questionnaires and interviews from newspapers and special interest groups, and many of them asked for a photo. I knew that the Chicago Sun-Times had at least one decent photo of me on file already, but they requested another to post online along with my answers to their questionnaire. In my hurry to get it out, I just clicked on the only headshot I had in my computer files (Laura usually sent the photos), sent it off to the paper and forgot about it. On the day it appeared on the net, a reader commented, "She looks like a skeleton from a video game. Well, a friendly one." The same picture was briefly posted on my website and, unfortunately, a blogger chose to review my site while the "skeleton" picture was there. His review wasn't so "friendly":

Oh my ~ And the photo that someone posted of her there, which looks like someone dressed as a witch for Halloween, has got to be either a really mean prank or a grand-kid that just thinks that Gramma always looks pretty.

I freely admit, I have never been very photogenic, but, *please...* The insult came in December and fortunately by that time, I had reached the point of proper perspective, and things like this no longer bothered me. I am fairly certain that had someone said I looked like a video game skeleton back at the beginning of the campaign, I would have thrown myself, skeleton and all, into a dark closet and refused to come out.

The first picture of me in the Springfield State Journal-Register was an unflattering candid shot. There was a strong wind on the day it was taken at the fair so my frizzy hair was out of control and I wore very little makeup. At least there were no references to Halloween in the article. After that picture appeared in the paper, Laura used my camera to take about thirty shots of me against the cornfield in our backyard, but I was not happy with any of them. Kristen Gustafson, a woman with an eye for what looks good, snapped another thirty shots indoors with her digital camera and came up with the photo we used for just about everything. It wasn't professional perfect, but it was me and we could all live with it.

The whole image thing was an issue from the start. On one of the first days in the tent at the State Fair a gentleman said to me, "It's nice to see a female candidate in a skirt." And Laura reported that when she pointed out to an elderly gentleman who I was, he questioned, "You mean the lady with the gray hair?!" My gray hair was a constant. At first, I did not intend to color it, but my volunteer staff (a.k.a. my friends) began to initially drop hints about it and finally flat out said that I had to get rid of the gray. In October I hit a compromise by having dark highlights put in, hoping to draw people's attention away from my hair and on to what I had to say. And still, after the color change, someone referred to me as the one with the "big hair."

I don't know exactly what a Republican looks like—or a Democrat for that matter—but apparently there is a look to define you as one or the other. The first time I was defined by the "look" was related to me by my husband, Dwight. He shared with me that one day he met two people and the conversation turned to politics. When he told them that I was running for the U.S. Senate they said that they had seen a red car around town with a *Kathleen Thomas for U.S. Senate* magnet stuck to the side. They looked in the car and saw a gray frizzy-haired driver and determined that she must be a Democrat. After googling my name they were surprised to find out that I was a Republican.

Jerry took us to the feed store and we met three guys there...one about 20, one about 30 and the other, 40. We chatted a minute and the oldest guy asked my stand on the 2nd amendment. I said pro-2nd amendment and, yes, I was for concealed carry. He immediately said I had his vote! Plus, he liked the fact that I wore jeans into the store.

Journal Entry-January 19

My resume, too, gave some people the impression that I was a liberal-thinking candidate. I'm not a lawyer, accountant, or realtor and I have never owned my own business—presumed professions of Republican candidates. I have a bachelor's degree in English and educational psychology, a master's degree in clinical psychology, and a doctorate in humanities. I have taught at several colleges and served on a local school board. More than once I was asked how I managed to be in academia and stay conservative. I described to one woman an incident that occurred while I was teaching at Florida State and Florida A&M. I wore sandals most of the time on campus and my hair has always been bushy and a little curly. One day one of my colleagues whom I had known for several years exclaimed that he had no idea I was politically conservative. And I said, "Why wouldn't you think I was?" And he said, "Well, you've got frizzy hair and you wear sandals and you work in academia." How interesting the way we judge and assume just from someone's appearance.

My clothes were another image issue I would have liked to ignore. I like to keep my wardrobe simple, classic and comfortable and I resisted changing my clothing style for the campaign. But some supporters thought I should dress differently. Many people viewed a YouTube video of me speaking to a 9/12 group at New Salem State Park. It was one of my first public speaking opportunities and it went very well. While I received a number of emails complimenting my astuteness of the subject matter, there was one gentleman who stated that I needed to dress more like his fifth grade teacher (whatever that meant!).

Kristen (remember, my photographer) swept several department stores to find clothes that would impress. She brought a mountain of blouses, slacks, sweaters and suits to my house for trying on. I rejected all but a couple of items. A week later she sent me to Macy's to try on "a few" suits she had picked out and set aside at the store. I approached a sales lady and began explaining who I was and why I was there. Before I finished she said, "Oh, yes, Dr. Thomas. You're running for the Senate. Please, follow me." She took me to the largest dressing room they had and I wondered if she heard me suck in my breath when she opened the door. There were not "several" items, there were more like "several" hundred! Shopping for clothes ranks right at the top of my list of things I dislike doing and just having to try them on without shopping for them did not sweeten the deal. I closed the door and plunged in. About two hours later I surfaced and had settled on one skirt and jacket, one pantsuit, and one top, all items I wore over and over again.

In the fall I met with the Sangamon County Republican interim chairperson, Rosie Long. I went to the headquarters, located across from the State Fairgrounds. I entered through the rear door and walked to the front of the building where Rosie was. As we entered the conference room, she said with feeling, "nice pantsuit, I really like it." I thanked her and we discussed some things I needed to do to have a legitimate campaign. She held out no hope that I had a chance of winning. She firmly believed the party choice would win. I agreed with her but said that if he did win, he would not win the general election.

The funny thing about pictures and makeup and clothes and hair dye is that up close and personal none of those things matter. During the last week of campaigning, Loretta (my sister), Laura and I drove up to Chicago to attend an event. We pulled into the parking lot of a McDonald's/gas station/convenience store so I could do a telephone interview with radio talk show host Bob Murray of Springfield. After the interview I went into the store to use their restroom. Spotting me, Loretta pulled me over to the McDonald's where six or seven men, possibly farmers, were chatting over coffee. I was in my usual travelling clothes of jeans and a loose-fitting sweater and my hair was clipped back off my makeup-less face. I introduced myself to the gentlemen, gave them each a business card and engaged them in a lively conversation about gun control and Mark Kirk's Yes vote on Cap and Trade, to which they were vehemently opposed. They were genuine and supportive of my candidacy and we even joked about my appearance. As we got ready to leave, one of the men said with much sincerity, "Thank you for doing what you are doing. I appreciate it."

For one endorsement session in Chicago, I arrived the night before and stayed at a hotel. I woke up early and couldn't go back to sleep and decided to get my shower when I realized I had forgotten all of my hair products, including my gel. This meant I would have to use the hotel shampoo or just wet my hair and hope for the best. Now, anyone that is attached to their hair products, as I am, knows what I'm talking about when I say I prefer my own routine. So I weighed the options and decided to just wet the hair. After the shower I realized I had forgotten my eye shadow and knee high hose. If I decided to wear slacks (which I did) I would have to go with full pantyhose, which is uncomfortable but would work. The hair looked actually pretty good and the pantyhose under the pantsuit felt uncomfortable but looked okay. Men just don't go through this. They shave, then ask "does this tie go?" and out the door!

On another trip to the Chicago area, and after the newspaper endorsement meeting with Southtown Star, my sister, Becky and I left for Middlebrook to go to Whole Foods and then to our hotel, where we pigged out on any and all kinds of food, including desserts and chocolate, throwing caution and calories to the wind. I had "pitted out" my only shirt so I hand-washed it in the sink. We then relaxed by watching *American Idol* and *The Simpsons* and wondered what Mark Kirk was doing. Laughing at ourselves, we asked, "Wonder if he's washing out *his* shirt?"

The time and effort put into our maintenance as women is funny to talk about in retrospect. Yet, the reality is that the time and thought we spend agonizing over our appearance is part of being female in a very visually critical world. How we look, how we dress, how we carry ourselves are all part and parcel of our objectification. In regard to gender, however, the real issue is that women's life experiences are different from those of men and yet we are not directly represented in government anywhere near proportion to our numbers. Conservative women especially, are under-represented. Women are at the center of the values we espouse—marriage being between a man and a woman, respect for life at all its stages, education of our children, and easing the tax burden on families. In an Op-Ed article by me and posted on RFFM.org (Republicans For Fair Media) I explained my belief that "the traditional family is being attacked on all sides. As a mother, a grandmother and American this is of great concern to me." If, as conservative Republicans, we believe and support traditional family values, we need to be serious about having conservative-thinking women in congress.

It is tough for women who want to run for office in the state of Illinois and even tougher for Republican women. On January 30th the Springfield State Journal-Register printed a story about diversity in the Primary. It broke down the make-up of the

We must elect conservative legislators who understand that everything that is decided in Washington impacts families. We must elect legislators who will work to keep the traditional family intact so that our nation will continue to rear generations of strong leaders who will fight to maintain the liberties we have.

Op Ed article-RFFM.org

Primary candidates by race and gender. There was nothing shocking or revealing about the article, but the online comments that were posted afterward generally indicated a naiveté among the public. Most of the comments spouted the ideal that anyone who wants to can run for office, which is true. They also said that voters look past color and gender and always vote for who they like best, which, in my experience, is not true. But only one reader suggested that candidates of a certain race or gender could be favored by the Parties in order to appeal to pockets of voters. Loretta Durbin, president of Illinois Women's Institute for Leadership, was quoted in the article as saying, "Statewide, I think it takes a long time for women to rise up the chain. I think you just have to pull more women into the system." It is curious to me that the percentage of women running in any campaign never even comes close to being proportionate to the total population, which is over fifty percent female.

My experience in Illinois politics is that the Republican Party neither adequately recruits nor grooms female candidates. Judy Barr Topinka, former Illinois State Treasurer, stands alone. I've heard people joke that the Illinois Republican Party has one female—Topinka—and they trot her out every now and then to run for something. During this election cycle she was running for Comptroller. I am convinced that there is a real need for more women to get directly involved by running for office, but I am also sure that, at present, the majority of women who do put themselves out there are not being embraced or taken seriously by Party leaders.

> *Be the kind of woman that when your feet hit the floor each morning the devil says--"Oh Crap, She's up!"*
>
> *Email message sent by Becky Hill-September 6*

I met only a handful of women on the campaign trail who were running for any office. In January, at a supper event sponsored by the Republican Women of Macomb, I found myself helping out in the serving line. While handing out sandwiches to hungry guests, I introduced myself to the woman who was standing next to me and discovered she was running for circuit judge. She told me that it was her opinion that the men would not let women in on the circuit. She explained that for years women had run every time there was an election but it was always a no go. She and others were frustrated that the network of men kept women from being taken seriously. I am not sure why the women do not win the elections; she gave no explicit reason, but I know for sure that there is a real frustration among female candidates. Is it that without Party backing your chances of winning an election are slim? Or, are these women just not running good campaigns? I think the former is true.

The idea of diversity among candidates was brought to light by my experience at the State Journal-Register endorsement meeting in Springfield. Don Lowery was sitting next to Mark Kirk and a reporter was asked a question about how we thought things should be handled in Iran. Lowery answered in a few sentences and then his comments devolved into a general discussion of the Middle East and his tour of duty in Vietnam. He said that our country is in trouble and "what is wrong with Congress is that there are not enough veterans; we need more veterans in Congress." It struck me that the African-American candidate had been touted as such, veterans had been mentioned and so I decided okay, let's talk about gender then. So when it came my time to speak I said, "It seems that if they're specifically mentioning veterans and African-American candidates, then I need to bring to attention the gender issue. We might need more veterans and African Americans but what about more women? Thirty to forty percent of the conservative voters are women and they are represented by two to three percent in the Senate. So, if we want to talk about what is wrong with this country, then let's mention the fact that conservative women are *grossly* underrepresented." There was no response or follow-up to my remarks from the editors and reporters in the room.

We met a few people who do vote along gender lines. Eighteen-year old Curtis went with us to gather signatures at the DuQuoin State Fair. He approached a gentleman and asked him for his signature and was taken aback when the man said, "I never vote for women." Curtis was in disbelief that anyone in 2010 could have such an attitude, and went on to ask again for his signature. "No, I never vote for women," he repeated. My son Joshua and his wife Courtney had a similar experience. Courtney, herself an independent, strong woman, approached a man who said, "I don't vote for women for anything". Courtney laughed thinking that he was joking so she asked him again if he would sign my petition. The man replied, "No, I'm serious, I don't vote for women under any circumstance."

On the flipside, after speaking to 300 Republicans at an event in Effingham, my sister, Loretta, overheard one woman turn to another and say, "A strong, powerful woman…I like her." When the event was over, a female mayor of a small town approached me and joking, yet serious, said, "I don't understand why they don't put women in charge of everything…we know how to manage money and we know how to shop for a bargain!"

On the way home from Johnston City I got a call from Lowery who filled me in on the latest gossip. According to him, Patrick Hughes had talked with John Arrington and asked him to bow out. John accused Hughes of being racist. Hughes also called Zadek who, upset, called Lowery. Lowery was calling me to tell me that one of Hughes' aides had gone to the State Board of Elections and copied all of our petitions and that I needed to stay in the race. I said there was never any question. I told Laura that I couldn't get out of the race now even if I wanted to because, if I did, the men would have a heyday…*Oh, yes, we knew the woman would drop out…most women can't take the heat*…blah, blah, blah.

These campaigning experiences reinforced all those clichés and caricatures about professional politicians. Some candidates, especially incumbents, were skilled at waffling, rationalizing, saying what the crowd wanted to hear, or being disingenuous. Some had their behavior down to an exact science—their answers were slick and their behavior never varied. It was evident which candidates were professional or had hired consultants to help them with their image. Patrick Hughes is a good example of this type of candidate. His clear straight-forward way of expressing himself changed after he began working with his paid consultant—and in my opinion, not for the better; his speeches had become rehearsed and canned. I heard may people say that he came across as impersonal and unlikable.

I believe that the life experience and perspective I would have brought to the Senate is greatly needed. But whether we elect women or men to that high office, I hope that they are true to their beliefs and principles. I am proud of the fact that I held firm to what I believed throughout the six months under a microscope. I did not have to worry about what I was or wasn't saying to this group or that, or this individual, or that newspaper, as I was saying the same thing to all. And I was saying the same thing because my words were grounded in what I believe. I discovered that if you have values that you are committed to you will not have a problem being consistent with your answers in varying situations. Maybe this is why it was so easy for me to meet and talk to people about the issues. This was the part of the campaign I enjoyed most of all.

People are paid big bucks for creating an image. But because I wasn't interested in pretending to be someone I am not, it really did not matter that I lacked the funds to pay a political consultant to define Kathleen Thomas. I believe that the real me was one of my greatest assets as a candidate. I felt great satisfaction on Election Day to read a second article written by the author of the "Halloween Witch Gramma" comment.

As for myself, I candidly will tell you that I made a choice to vote for Kathleen Thomas for US Senator... Kathy may or may not turn out to be all I hoped for, but I can tell you that she really seems to care. She cared enough to personally respond to emails I sent her that she could have chosen not to answer. Tough emails concerning issues that are hot-button and important to me and America... Tough issues like abortion and gay marriage...

-Plainfield Today, February 2, 2010

Interviews and Issues

I could just drive to Mexico…

At first, interviews were the most excruciating part of campaigning, which is rather ironic since they eventually became one of my favorite things to do. Radio interviews in particular turned out to be the most enjoyable. I preferred them over television or newspaper interviews, questionnaires, or phone interviews. With radio I didn't have to worry so much about my "image," and I could have notes in front of me. My first radio interview was at WTAX in Springfield, and it preceded any other large public function. I was painfully nervous when I pulled into the radio station parking lot and I seriously entertained the thought…*I could just drive to Mexico and never look back and no one would ever find me.* But I didn't. I went in and, fortunately, for my first interview I could not have asked for a nicer host, Bob Murray. The interview focused more on who I was and why I was running rather than the issues. I was grateful for this because I was still in the process of learning about the issues and how to properly articulate my view of them. Some radio interviews were conducted over the phone out of convenience to me; still, I definitely preferred going to the studio for a face-to-face interview. Of course, the more I was interviewed the easier it became. By the end of the campaign I could rattle off answers confidently and knowledgably. I still am amazed at the difference between my first and last interviews, how much more I knew and how relaxed I was toward the end.

My first television interview was with UnaVision Channel 66 on a bitterly cold and gray day in December. Laura Gough and I drove to Chicago and I pulled into the parking lot across from the station. I started to drive down an aisle, looking for a parking space, when I heard someone yelling at me. A wiry middle-aged man was giving me the what for and pointing to a sign that said "Stop At Window First," which I hadn't up to this point seen. I pulled back and rolled down my window and he read me the riot act again about not seeing that sign that was right in my face, etc, etc. I said, very calmly, "well you've got to be patient with us girls from the country; I didn't see that sign, sorry." He softened a little. "Well," he said, "if you had parked here without stopping at my window, you'd have to pay $170." "Thanks for saving us from that," I responded. "How much is it to park?" As I got out of the car to hand him a twenty I thanked him again for helping us and chatted with him a little. He was nice as could be by the time I walked away. Laura said, "I can't believe you did that. I would have crawled under my seat, in tears! You totally changed him around." I figured he was used to dealing with people giving tit for tat all the time and he was probably surprised when I didn't.

At the station, an assistant took us into a studio where we waited for about thirty minutes, giving us time to thaw out because it felt as though the wind chill factor had dropped the temperature to single digits. I wasn't too nervous for this interview since it was taped. Paula, a gracious woman whom I learned was from Miami, and originally from Columbia, took me back for the interview. I was offered a bottle of water and they decided my face needed some make-up. The interview began with extremely long involved questions that I think she lifted from the internet. She spoke rapidly and rather softly, with her face down, reading the questions and I struggled just to understand what she was saying. There were facts and figures and mention of some bills I had heard of but did not know their details. I listened intently and was able to apply my basic philosophical principles and give answers. I felt most comfortable with the healthcare and economy questions and least comfortable with the question about immigration. After the interview, the cameraman had me walk down the hall both ways while he filmed me. They said they would use pieces of that in the segment.

My second television interview was short and also taped. It was with a Chicago NBC affiliate and my sister Becky was with me. I arrived a little early and was able to take John Arrington's spot because he was running late, as usual! After a few issue questions, such as gays in the military and how to create more jobs, I was then asked about the most recent movie I had seen, book I had read and what type of car I drove. Of course my mind went blank for a second about the movie, but then it came to me...*The Blind Side*. It was a rather pleasant, short interview.

The third interview was a whole different ballgame as it was to be aired live during the noon news hour. Becky was also with me for this interview. We drove to our usual parking lot in downtown Chicago and sat in the car while I put on make-up and fixed my hair when I said, "let's go ahead and walk there because the wind is going to blow my hair anyway." So we walked to the Tribune building and into the WGN Radio station and realized we were at the wrong address. The receptionist told us the TV station was across town and, because of the distance, we definitely couldn't walk...we would have to drive. So Becky, who does *not* like driving when there is lots of traffic, is at the wheel in downtown Chicago driving like a maniac. She ran a stop sign (accidentally), did a u-turn under an overpass (and almost hit a car in the process) because we had gone in the wrong direction, probably drove too fast, but, by golly, she got me there on time! They took us into a waiting room, brought us bottled water and a technician came and miked me and we waited. And waited…and waited. I could hear Becky talking but I was not listening. I turned and said to her, "water, I need water." The program director finally came and showed us into the studio and that's when it hit me that I was nervous because this was a *live* interview. During a pause in the show, they ushered me onto the stage and all of a sudden, as I sat down next to the two anchor people, I felt empowered and thought *this will be fun*. Everyone that saw it said I did a great job.

After we left I felt as if I had a new lease on life! We changed our clothes in the car and headed home. We started eating some of the delicious food we had bought at Whole Foods earlier that day…sweet potatoes, clam chowder, cornbread, yummy parfaits and various chocolates! Becky drove most of the way back to Springfield and I drove the last bit, all the while making calls and organizing. When we arrived home I was so tired I could hardly think. I sent off the final Tribune questionnaire and we worked on the Abigail Adams questionnaire. I dropped in bed about eleven thirty and was asleep by eleven thirty-one.

A large portion of my time during the late fall and early winter was spent answering questionnaires, which is actually just another form of interviewing. From newspapers like the Chicago Tribune to smaller publications and special interest groups such as the NRA, Right to Life, NARAL, various Environmental groups, Union and Right to Work groups, etc., there was no end to the different organizations that wanted to know my stand, and how I would benefit their cause. All of my answers would appear in print or somewhere online. Although it was an incredible amount of work, I realize that the process I went through in responding to these questionnaires was crucial in helping me solidify my thoughts on specific issues. I am fiscally conservative and believe that legislation should be grounded in the Constitution, but having to answer the large number of questions that came from these publications and organizations helped me articulate with greater specificity than had previously been required. Consequently, I was better prepared to speak at the 9/12, Tea Party, and Republican Party forums. I began the campaign with strong opinions about Cap and Trade and Health Care and in the end I could voice, with conviction, my stand on issues such as Second Amendment rights, Middle East involvement, education, etc. One questionnaire I received was over one hundred questions in length. Some groups, especially the newspaper print media asked me to limit my response to one hundred fifty to two hundred fifty words; some wanted even less. I became very good at giving concise answers. The Tea Party and 9/12 groups also had some form of questionnaire. A few had statements that they wanted the candidates to sign, declaring our beliefs. It was really a contract, stating that if we were elected and we did not uphold the Constitution and conservative values, they would do everything in their power to remove us.

When I attended the forums of the different organizations, I always took questions from the audience. In *general*, the members of the Tea Party and 9/12 groups were the most politically astute and their questions reflected this. They showed a sound understanding of the Constitution, the political process and current issues. The people at the gun organizations were well aware of legislation in general and acutely aware of the legislation that personally affected them and their gun ownership. People at the Republican Party events asked questions of a more soft-ball nature and seemed most concerned with how much money I had/could raise and what kind of campaign network I had. There were, however, some very politically astute Republicans who showed a genuine concern about the issues (Palatine Township being one) and then there were those townships that wanted to see the money and the organization (Libertyville and Barrington come to mind.).

Came home and finished filling out questionnaire #3,000. At least that is what it seems like. Interesting how each specific special interest group words their questions to lead you to the way they want you to answer.

No matter what type of media I was engaged with, there was always the risk of being quoted out of context, creative editing of an interview, taking a quote and splitting it so it would sound different and just plain getting it wrong. In a phone interview for a newspaper publication, I was asked if I believed terrorism was real. I replied, "I believe that there is definitely a faction of the population in the world that wants us dead, and it doesn't matter what we say or do." When I saw the final interview, I was appalled. They printed that I had said "The Islamic faith views us as a corrupt nation and we can't change that perception." Now, if the misquote was unintentional, then we are talking, at worst, some sloppy, poor journalism. If it was an intentional misquote, that falls into another category entirely, one that is extremely scary. Once you have given an interview, you have no control over what the media does with it.

In another interview I was asked why I was running for the Senate. Why didn't I start smaller and work my up? I replied with, "Why not? There are over 1,500 years of experience in the Senate right now," I said, "and we're probably in more trouble than we have ever been." When the reporter from the Chicago Tribune wrote the story, he said that when I was asked why I was starting with a Senate race as my first political race I responded with "Why not?" The rest of my answer was separated from those two words, making my response sound flippant! The impression and the damage were already done. It might seem like splitting hairs with these examples, but it does matter and it does make a difference when the public is trying to become informed. I was in a catch-22 in that I didn't have the money to buy the publicity that would give me the name recognition I needed, so I accepted all the free less-than-perfect publicity I could get. Voters who were diligent and really wanted to know what the candidates stood for usually attended the forums, called me, or in some way tried to make contact to determine what it was I really believed and stood for.

Although I was largely left to my own conservative principles and research devices when generating opinions on policy or answers to the numerous questions I received, I was grateful to my campaign manager who helped by finding articles for me. My brother Wesley, who is a lawyer and worked for the Heritage Foundation, was also an enormously helpful resource.

What I found most interesting was that when I would come to a conclusion or write what I thought would be a good solution after having done the research, it was usually the exact same concept or idea that Congressman Boehner, the House Minority Leader would send out in his weekly email addresses, sometimes with even the same wording! I believe this is further proof that an ordinary citizen could step up and do this job of being a Congressional Representative or Senator. I've heard congressmen/women sound like idiots when they're being interviewed. Do not think for a minute that they are any smarter than the rest of us, they just have experience, (e.g....they've been there a long time) and a lot of staff members to help them research and stay abreast of the issues. Any one of you reading this book, grounded in principles, could do the job of an elected official.

Endorsements

Well, it's not an exact science.

One great disappointment was the editorial board endorsements from the major newspapers. For those unfamiliar with this process, let me explain. Newspapers' editorial boards interview the candidates individually and determine who will make the best elected official. At least in theory this is the way it is supposed to work. I was interviewed over the phone for at least one endorsement, a newspaper in Moline, where the board gathered around a speaker phone and asked their questions. I was interviewed by other publications in person.

Andy Martin, Don Lowery, nor I were invited to the *Chicago Tribune* endorsement. (Andy Martin had committed political suicide with his radio ads and had become toxic. He was pretty much shunned from December 28th on). Mark Kirk, Patrick Hughes, and John Arrington were the only candidates invited to the *Chicago Tribune* endorsement session. I called the paper and asked why. Pat Widder, one of the editors, said, "Well, we consulted with political consultants and looked at those that had answered our questionnaire, and, well, it's not an exact science. I'm sorry if you feel slighted, and we will set up an appointment with you at a later date." The solution didn't seem complicated at all—just invite all of the candidates.

I later learned that John Arrington had not submitted answers to the Tribune's questionnaire and *he* (John) said that the only reason he was invited to the endorsement session was because he was Black. My best guess is that they had already decided on Mark Kirk and, to make it look legitimate, they had to invite a few more candidates. It was convenient (and politically expedient) to invite the Black man and the other guy from Chicago. The Tribune, it seemed to me, was not worried about the woman (me) and the judge (Don Lowery) from Southern Illinois. I am sure they thought we were non-players with no power to negatively impact the Tribune or to let the electorate know what was going on. But, of course, the voters never knew any of this and all they saw and heard was that the Tribune endorsed Kirk.

The *Southtown Star Gazette* (a paper at Tinley Park in the Southern suburbs of Chicago) also held an endorsement session. My sister Becky and I arrived about 10 minutes early. We sat in the Lobby and watched the others approach. Don

Worked for hours on the Tribune questionnaire. It was all about foreign relations...North Korea, Iran, Afghanistan and the Middle East. You know, simple, bumper sticker type questions and answers. I could've written pages on just one of those countries...what with history, pros and cons. I mean, there is no consensus among the "experts" on foreign affairs. So I attempted to read them all and couple it with my common sense.

Journal Entry-December 17

Lowery arrived after me. Apparently, this newspaper invited all of the candidates. I felt they had called us all there to make it appear legitimate once they picked Kirk to endorse. Did they think we were idiots? At a few minutes before 4:00, Kirk's young assistant drove up in a car and then Kirk and his driver drove up in their large van. The assistant got out of his car and went into the van where they waited for about 10 minutes. The contact lady came and got Lowery and me and took us back for our pictures. After my picture was taken, Kirk, who had been in the parking lot for fifteen minutes, walked in—maybe he wanted a grand entrance, but little did he realize that the perennially late John Arrington had yet to show.

Don Lowery's behavior toward Kirk surprised me. At the beginning of the campaign, during the months of September and October, he talked about how he despised Kirk—how Kirk must be defeated. But now he seemed a little obsequious. He apologized to Kirk concerning Andy Martin's negative radio ads. Don Lowery is a nice guy—polite to everyone—but he was going overboard with Kirk at this meeting. He looked at Kirk and gestured toward the photographer, "You go first." "No," said Kirk, "You go first." Lowery responded, "No, please, you go first." After a few more times of this, I couldn't stand it anymore and said, impatiently, "Just go in Judge!" It was as if he were actually impressed with being in Kirk's presence. This was not the Don Lowery I had grown to know and admire on the campaign trail

We entered the conference room and I said in my mind, "Let the games begin!" Mark Kirk walked by me and placing his hand on my shoulder, smoothly asked "Kathy, can I get you some water?" He was extremely polished. The editor, publisher, reporters, and associate editors were there. We were asked questions and they rotated who would answer first, etc. At one point Kirk said that the Senate was not an entry level job. When asked why he thought he should be the Senator, he said he had $3 million and the endorsement of the Tribune. When it was over, Becky and I walked out of the room. I turned to Lowery and said, "Judge, if they don't endorse you, I'll be really surprised." I felt almost cruel saying this because, as well as the Judge had done, (and it was one of his better jobs), I knew in my heart they had already selected Kirk.

In January, I phoned the *State Journal-Register* in Springfield about their editorial board endorsement. Eric, Kirk's campaign manager, had called me earlier that week and left a message that the *State Journal Register* was having an endorsement session and inviting only Kirk and Hughes and he said that Kirk wanted me to be aware of this. I called the State Journal-Register and spoke with Matthew Dietrich, Editorial Page Editor, who said that that was not the case at all; nothing had been decided yet and, in fact, they had been thinking that they might send out a survey, instead of holding a meeting. When I hung up and looked at Laura we both laughed…"someone's lying" she said. I guess Kirk wanted the rest of the candidates to know about the endorsement so he would appear magnanimous, or because he feared a race between just himself and Hughes. It could be he wanted all the candidates present at the endorsement sessions to make his (Kirk's) endorsement look more legitimate. Or, maybe it was some of all of the above.

The actual endorsement session proved even more interesting than the lead-up to it. Mark Kirk was aggressively confronted by Patrick Hughes about his No vote on banning partial birth abortion. Kirk gave a very disingenuous answer saying he was personally opposed to partial birth abortion but did not want to go against the law of the land or the Supreme Court. I wanted to jump up and scream…"What does that mean?! You're against something but you vote for it? We don't want politicians like that anymore." I don't think Kirk understood that the job of a legislator is to create legislation in keeping with his conscience and let the Supreme Court determine whether or not it is constitutional. As I see it, if he was honestly "personally opposed to partial birth abortion," then he was just kowtowing to the editorial board and trying to be all things to all people, saying he was opposed to it while voting for it. None of the editorial board questioned him on his illogical argument. Kirk also said he supported the 2nd amendment. None of the board pursued this by asking him why, if he did support the 2nd amendment, did he have a grade of F from the NRA? (The National Rifle Association grades members of Congress on their voting record as it pertains to their support of the Second Amendment and they scored Mark Kirk with a grade of "F".) When asked if he supported concealed carry, he responded with "It never comes up on the floor of the Senate." When asked two more times the same question, he gave the same answer. The reporter finally stopped asking the question, and that was that.

Kirk also stated he was for tax cuts, but no one asked him why, then, had he voted Yes for Cap and Trade, potentially the biggest tax hike in American history. Again, the *State Journal-Register* editorial board did not drill down. It seemed we were merely going through the motions. When asked what his credentials were, Kirk responded, as he had at the *Southtown Star*, with "four million dollars" and "the endorsement of the Chicago Tribune." Maybe the editorial board, not wishing to appear provincial and out of touch, endorsed the same person the *Tribune* endorsed.

In fairness to the *State Journal-Register*, I spoke with one of the reporters the day before the election. He had attended the endorsement session but was not a member of the editorial board. I asked him why no one had questioned Mark Kirk in depth. He said, and I applaud his honesty, that the editorial board probably did not know what Kirk was talking about and did not fully understand his voting record or his grade of F with the NRA.

I learned, after talking with several political operatives, that it was very unusual to interview the candidates all at the same time. Normally they are interviewed on an individual basis. Newspaper interviews done over the phone were, by their very nature, one on one. Why was protocol ignored? Were the newspapers just going through the motions?

I gave short, succinct, and common sense answers. I gave answers, the men gave rhetoric...on and on and on! Mark had mentioned at Southtown "this was not an entry level job" and I agree with him. What we disagree on are the requirements for the job. He apparently thinks that money and endorsements and 12 years in the house are the qualifications for the job

Journal Entry-January 15

Some of the local party organizations held endorsement sessions also. The endorsements at the township level were held at some location such as a Civic Center or church or at the local Republican Party headquarters, as was the case with Libertyville.

The candidates waited in one area and then we were called into the endorsement session one at a time. At some of these sessions we were allowed to bring someone in with us, at others we were not.

At Libertyville I was asked, "Is this your campaign slogan, 'Do Something Different'?" "Yes," I responded. "I am offering something different for the people--a conservative woman. I had no intention of calling attention to gender when I entered the race, but many people wanted to vote for me even before they knew exactly where I stood on the issues just because I'm a woman." I told the board I was smart and conservative and I hoped they would take that into consideration first. I also explained that people signed my petition *because* I didn't have political experience. "There are a lot of people who just don't want Kirk," I said. "They're very angry at his Cap and Trade vote." One gentleman pointed out that I had been on a school board. "You're right," I said. "Yes, I was elected to the school board and served four years. We built a green school and came in under budget!" A lady asked about marriage—what I thought traditional marriage was. I explained that I believe everyone has civil rights, but marriage is between a man and a woman. A guy sitting next to her said, "Well, since she opened the door... what is your favorite caliber?" "A 45," I answered, "because it has a nice kick!" They all laughed. Some liked me, but I had no delusion—I knew they would support Kirk because of the money, and same-old, same-old.

The Ford County Republicans had an evening endorsement session at Gibson City that I attended after having been to a Republican meeting in Champaign. The session was held in the basement of a bank and I had been previously told by the county chairman, Eric Thompson, that I could bring yard signs. I arrived at the bank and carried my signs in. There were several local candidates, a Lt. Governor candidate, myself, and a young guy representing Mark Kirk. I thought the session went well. I fielded questions and seemed to get a lot of positive response and heads nodding "yes". When no one from Gibson City had called me by mid-morning of the next day I knew who they had endorsed. I called Eric Thompson and, as I suspected, they endorsed Kirk. I asked what they were looking for in a candidate. He said, "Well, money and name recognition".

"So, the fact that he is a liberal doesn't matter?" I queried.

"He's also got the backing of the National Party and they have endorsed him and will continue   to help in the general election. Well, he is going to realize that he doesn't have just one liberal group (his Congressional District on Chicago's north shore) but he must go statewide, he will have   to   be   more moderate." (So what Eric is saying is that he thinks Mark Kirk is so liberal that   he is going to have to come back to center to even attempt to appeal to conservatives!)

"But a vast number of people want a conservative, and they don't want someone that voted Yes for Cap and Trade," I pressed. "So what you're saying is that the Party is an end in itself, not a   means to an end. You're saying that the Party decides who will win the primary." (It has never occurred to him, I guess, that if in the Primary the people are allowed to elect who *they* want, the chances of that person beating the Democrat nominee are greater than if the Party picks the person.)

"Well, not exactly."

"But if they send the same-old, same-old they will get the same-old, same-old. Nothing is going   to change. He will be just like the others…unresponsive to the people because he cares more about his job than the people." No response. "Well, thank you for inviting me, even though you knew the outcome."

"Well, now, not really. I've told him (Kirk) that he's got to watch it if he wants to stay in office. It isn't going to be easy to win." There was a slight pause and then he said, "Oh, you've got some signs here."

"Yes, I told the people in Champaign I'd bring some over to them…I'll be up there at some point   to pick them up and take them over there."

"I can get them over there for you, I know exactly who is going and can take them for you." I thanked him and thought that the person taking my signs was probably someone at the meeting that wanted to endorse me, and possibly stood up against the supporters of Kirk.

Local Party endorsements are part of the political game. Sangamon County (where my hometown of Springfield is located) chose not to endorse anyone and I told Toni Libri, the Republican County Chair, that I thought that was a wise decision. I can't help but wonder, are Party leaders not concerned with the personal integrity of a person and his or her core beliefs? It seems the incumbent candidate's motivation is to keep the job and will therefore do what must be done to keep the party happy. Eric Thompson confirmed that. But Party endorsement sessions were always a disappointment to me because, no matter how well I was received, no matter how much I was applauded, Mark Kirk always waltzed in with his millions of dollars and title and walked away with the endorsement. I was disappointed because, of course, I believed I was the better candidate. And as far as the money and organization…I was convinced it would come after the Primary.

The Independence Caucus invited me to participate in a vetting process where they would choose a conservative candidate to back. As far as I know, John Arrington, Don Lowery, and I were the only participants. I filled out and sent in a 105 question form and then had an hour long interview via conference call. The interview covered topics from fiscal responsibility to ethics, and most questions were centered on the Constitution. They asked if I would be able to withstand the pressure and the mudslinging that would take place in the general campaign. I replied that that would be the easy part of the campaign, and no, it wouldn't bother me. All of my children were grown adults with children of their own and they could handle any media scrutiny or pressure that my candidacy might bring. Our interviews were sent out to all the caucus members who then voted for the candidate they preferred. Lacking a front runner after the initial vote, a second vote was needed between Lowery and me. I was disappointed that I was not chosen, but of all the candidates, the Judge and I were most closely aligned philosophically. Their endorsement came a few weeks before the Primary, which seemed belated.

I believe that the National Republican Party and the Illinois Republican Party came rather late to the realization that there was a significant conservative ground swell, and either they chose to do nothing about it or they didn't know what to do about it. There were 321,893 out of 742,266 voters who did *not* vote for Kirk in the Primary, but chose to vote for one of the conservatives that were running. This is no small number and at some level the implications of this have to be acknowledged and addressed. The state Party, of late, has sought and promoted "moderate" candidates, which seems to me to be a contradiction of its very conservative 2008 platform (see addendum 3). In fact, the platform reads like a document produced by the conservative Tea Party movement.

> "As I have come to know Kathleen over the past five years, she has quickly grown in my respect. She is a hard working, knowledgeable, honest and caring public servant who truly believes in government that really is of the people, by the people and for the people. She won't rest until she thoroughly understands the issues and she listens to her constituents. As much as I enjoy having her as a neighbor here at home, I really want to see her in Washington. Let's try something new. Putting an honest, knowledgeable and hard working public servant in the Senate just might work for Illinois!"
>
> F. G. "Woody" Hester, M.A. FACHE, SPHR, Sr. Vice President & Chief People Officer Memorial Health System

-----

Endorsements are peculiar things. Political parties and special interest groups give endorsements and sometimes financial support if they think you will represent their interests. During a *Primary* campaign, endorsements are, or should be, taken with a grain of salt. During this Primary there were four true conservative candidates —Arrington, Lowery, Hughes and me. Patrick Hughes got the most endorsements because (1) he actively sought them (2) he told everyone that he was the only conservative candidate and people believed him, (3) he was willing to sink more of his own money ($250,000) into his campaign than the rest of us (a determining factor for many individuals and special interest groups that endorse), and (4) he used the word "endorse" very loosely. It was effective campaigning for sure, yet something of which voters should be more conscious.

Two "conversations" with a Sean Hannity Show screener illustrate how endorsements are often taken more seriously by the electorate than the ones doing the actual endorsing. Sean Hannity had mentioned on his radio show that Hughes was the only conservative candidate running in the Illinois U.S Senate Primary. Upon hearing this, my sister Becky, got on her phone immediately and tried to get through to say that wasn't true, that there were three other conservative candidates. She was successful in reaching the screener.

Screener: *Hannity Show*

Becky: *Hannity just said Patrick Hughes was the only conservative running and that's just not true.*

Screener: *Well, that's his opinion…*

Becky: *But…*

Screener: *It's his show...click.*

(On the same day I attempted to get through with the same message.)

Screener: *Looking for Obama supporters.*

Me: *Looking for Obama supporters?*

Screener: *Yes*

Me: *Well, I'm a Senate candidate from Illinois and...*

Screener: *Call back tomorrow...click*

Tomorrow was the day *after* the election. When I hung up I thought, "How can I believe anything from anyone? Who is a reliable source for political information?" Conservative talk show hosts will say that it is not their job to tell us who to vote for, but if the information they share in regard to an election is not complete, many of their listeners will not dig deeper to get the full story. In fairness, the Hannity Show was not the only radio talk show that jumped on the Hughes wagon without acknowledging the other conservative candidates. Mark Levin and Laura Ingram endorsed Patrick Hughes as the "only" conservative candidate from Illinois, verbiage straight from the Hughes campaign. The truth is he was the only conservative candidate from Illinois who was buying his way into the public eye with his own money. To the best of my knowledge and to their credit, Rush Limbaugh and Glenn Beck did not make any endorsements in the Illinois Senate Primary race.

One voter told me that he didn't vote for me because I did not have any endorsements listed on the home page of my website. True—I chose not to do that. What I did have posted on my home page were testimonials from people who had known me for years. I thought that this would effectively resonate with people. While Patrick Hughes was running around begging endorsements from people and organizations at every turn, I felt that the approval I had—that of real people who really knew and respected me—was of superior worth. New Berlin Superintendent of Schools, Valerie Carr, for example, wrote "I firmly believe that Kathleen Thomas is the right woman for the job. Her decisions on the school board were thoughtful, always made in the best interest of students, and always based on facts

> *"I have known Kathleen Thomas for 10 years. She is the rarest of people...highly intelligent and well informed, yet she has maintained her common sense. While empathetic and sincere, she has not lost her sense of humor. She also understands that our government was intended to represent the people, not create an overwhelming and out of touch bureaucracy. A vote for Kathleen Thomas is a vote for someone who will be a representative of the people, not another politician seeking career advancement."*   *-Chet Rhodes*

and preparation. We would be fortunate to have her in Congress. Please know she has my respect and my support."

Unfortunately, most voters were not willing to expend the time and the energy in the very arduous task of researching the many candidates on the ballot in this Primary election. Even some people who supported me asked me who they should vote for in the other races. One thing I learned throughout this campaign is that touting endorsements might be superficial, but when you are running for office, it does matter. Many People are impressed by who says they like you. It is, essentially, a popularity contest in the end –and you can buy popularity with money.

Growing Support

Wave at us Kathleen, so we can see who you are!

I would guess that less than a thousand people in the State of Illinois had heard of me before August, making name recognition my greatest challenge. Long before I filed my petition, I had envisioned the campaign as a flurry of hundreds of non-stop speaking engagements. From the start, organizations would clamor to have the candidates speak at their functions—all the Rotary Clubs, Kiwanis, educational organizations, coal mines, farmer's groups, etc. I assumed people would be curious to hear what I had to say about things. What I miscalculated was that not many people think about the Primary election five months prior. It was hard work during those first few months seeking out opportunities to meet and speak with voters and push myself in front of key people in the Republican Party.

My volunteer staff spent hours searching the internet for fall festivals and parades for us to attend. Connie, a contact in the Peoria area, told us about the Pekin Marigold parade scheduled for September twelfth. She got us registered to walk in the parade and encouraged us to purchase balloons with my name on them. She said that Aaron Schock (U.S. Representative for Illinois District 18) had used this strategy in the last election and put a balloon in the hands of every child watching the parade. On the surface the task seemed easy enough. Someone agreed to order the balloons and find the helium to inflate five hundred of them. So many little decisions needed to be made in a short period of time—what color balloons? What size? What color print? How do we transport the helium?

The balloons arrived late afternoon the day before the parade, but helium had become scarce, making it both expensive and difficult to find. Our options included spending two hundred forty-five dollars to rent a tank from a party store, or a refill service costing ninety dollars per month; neither of which were good options with our limited funds. We picked up the last three, small, twenty dollar tanks available in Springfield, and Laura brought a red wagon to haul them in during the parade. Within a block and a half we ran out of helium; two more blocks and we were out of candy. So, we passed out a couple hundred business cards. When we ran out of them, we handed out the limp unfilled balloons figuring parents would blow them up at some point and see my name printed on them. By the end of the parade we were hot and sweaty and lacked enthusiasm for collecting signatures at the festival.

Though exhausting and full of blunders, we decided that the parade was worthwhile—in two hours time, several thousand people saw me and my name. So, on October third we borrowed a little blue pickup truck from my neighbor to drive in the Barry Apple Festival parade. By this time I owned car magnets and a parade banner that read "Do Something Different" with my website. Before the parade began, we gathered signatures at the festival and filled and passed out helium balloons to the children waiting along the parade route.

We realized that at the Pekin parade we had wasted a great opportunity to fill pages of the petition. This time we had four volunteers go ahead of the parade to get signatures from the waiting crowd. By the time we rolled by with candy and stickers, almost every person watching the parade had heard of Kathleen Thomas. At the grandstand the announcer shouted, "Kathleen Thomas!…wave at us Kathleen, so we can see who you are." All in all, we gave away around 100 balloons, four pails of candy, a few hundred stickers, hundreds of business cards, and collected five hundred signatures.

…so we've got 5 kids and 6 adults…Ed and Colleen carry the banner and then the two Lauras and myself walk behind …the kids carry the candy…then Josh is driving the pick-up. It goes well…the people are so friendly. A person from the sidelines yelled, "I signed your petition at the tent at the State Fair". Another one said, "I signed your petition here". A group sitting in lawn chairs as I passed out my cards asked, "What party are you?" I said a conservative running on the republican ticket. They cheered and then I said, "And I vote NO to cap and trade!" They really cheered then!

Journal Entry-October 3

Late in August, I went to my first speaking engagement. Sherryl Clark was a recently active politico who learned about me at the State Fair. She single-handedly organized this and other meetings to inform people about what is happening in government. The meeting was held in my own town of Springfield, but because being late to anything makes me really tense and stressed I picked Laura up forty-five minutes early. Within minutes we proceeded to get lost. Fortunately, only Laura knew how tense I was as I rarely outwardly showed my anxiety or nervousness. We stopped at the only business we could find open, a pub, where Laura ran in and got directions. We continued on, arriving at our destination with 10 minutes to spare! All of my stress for naught!

There were only 12 people at the event and the meeting lasted an hour. Sherryl unnecessarily apologized for the poor attendance. As time went on, I realized that twelve is a pretty good number for a meeting of that kind. First up on the agenda that day were State Senator Larry Bomke and State Representative Raymond Poe who spoke and then left. The Senator and Representative droned on, and I got the last 5 minutes. My brief time was a perfect end to the meeting because I said exactly what I had to say and no more. They loved my message...they loved it because they could see that I was genuinely one of them and what I said was what they were thinking! I mentioned to the audience that they needed to pay close attention to their state legislators because, as I saw it, most government control needs to be given to the states; I told them that I would love to see the Federal government do only what the Constitution allows it to do. I went on to say that, given the opportunity, I would say No to Cap and Trade, No to HR 3200, and pretty much No to everything that isn't allowed by the Constitution. The first question I fielded was "how can we help you?" I told them to get signatures on my petition, and, as much as I did not like it, the reality was, I needed money to get my name out to the people of Illinois.

I truly appreciated Sherryl's enthusiasm and concern about the country. She invited me to a second meeting where she had a notary on hand for people to get my petitions notarized and returned to me. Sherryl and her husband, Jerry, were the couple who parked their RV in front of the State Board of Elections building the night before I filed the petition. Throughout my six months of campaigning, Sherryl frequently sent me encouraging emails which always seemed to come when I was feeling discouraged. She and Jerry were solid Americans and indicative of the new citizen—active, informed, and fearless!

Laura contacted several College Republican groups to see if they were interested in having me speak to them. We carefully planned our first speaking engagement at Bradley University. We had printed off a map and driving directions and packed, in the trunk of my car, a box full of t-shirts, stickers, pocket Constitutions, bumper stickers, and other campaign literature. We arrived early to make sure we would find the building in time and locate the room. We observed that the students were still having the business part of their meeting...I was the entertainment. We waited outside the room for them to finish and then walked in. The president of the group introduced me and, at ease in a college classroom setting, I addressed the fifteen young adults.

The college crowds were always interesting and I never quite knew how they would react. Some from the Black Hawk College were delighted to see a woman running and one young man said, right after hearing me speak, that he was voting for me. He was delighted to see someone different. For the most part, the college crowd was serious and well versed on the issues. Most of them were interested in hearing what I had to say, even if they were just there for extra credit.

Several people jumped on the Kathleen Thomas bandwagon early and gave the needed impetus to jump start the campaign. They worked in our basement headquarters at Laura Gough's house almost every night in September and October. One woman, Laura Bridges (L.B.), was especially dedicated. She worked long hours at her job all day and then came to work on the campaign late into the night. She also traveled with me to events in Chicago on several occasions. She knew how to work a crowd and was excellent with introductions. She seemed to know everyone in Springfield and was eager to have me meet people. Unfortunately, L B. moved out of state to a new job opportunity with about two months left in the campaign.

Ryan Flannagan was another invaluable volunteer during the beginning months. His suggestions headed us in the right direction when it came to finding speaking engagements and he was adept at computer research. Ryan was a great help at the Peoria parade and went with L.B. and me to a Republican dinner in DeKalb. Angie and Mike Winters were willing to do whatever we asked them, from clerical work to cooking pancakes. Other volunteers would come and go. Remember that all of these people, including my campaign manager, were not paid anything. They were all volunteers and without their efforts and grassroots enthusiasm I would not have even made the filing deadline.

Will go to Laura's at 6 for a campaign meeting. We are small but intense. Decided to spend our money on signs and on radio spots.

Journal Entry- November 6

It is tempting now to list and pay tribute to every person who helped us, but suffice it to say that my friends, family, and people who know me well enough to believe in me were the backbone of my campaign, emotionally, physically, and monetarily. Every bit of their help was important to me—from the "you go, girl", to stuffing envelopes, to the money they gave. My first monetary contribution was one thousand dollars from a good friend. Several days after handing me her generous check she called and said, "You can do this…it just dawned on me that you can do this!" They were the exact encouraging words I needed on a day when I was feeling blue and hoping for some help. My uncle, Ron Ockey, a former State Senator in another state sent me an inspiring note along with a sizable check. He advised me to spend my time studying the issues and preparing speeches. "Let the staff do everything else," he suggested. Little did he know my full time staff consisted of one person! But she worked as hard as I did, every day, all day, usually doing the work of a staff of 10.

I want to mention the invaluable campaigner my husband Dwight was. His was an unusual way of campaigning. He travels a lot to Florida for his job as a football recruiter. On his weekly trips he would give my campaign business card to bus and taxi drivers, the person he sat next to at the airport, the person he bought food from, and the person he sat next to on the airplane. He knows just about every coach in Florida and told all of them about me, and, invariably, the coaches would have family or friends or both that lived in Illinois. And if the coach didn't, then his wife did. I was amazed at how many people said they would contact their Illinois acquaintances. There was always a weekly story… a lady who was going to tell her reading group about me or someone who took a stack of cards to put in her place of business, etc. I wonder just how many votes I owe to Dwight's efforts!

I understood from the beginning that I would have to spend a great deal of time campaigning in Chicago. On October tenth, the Hispanic Republicans held a petition drive in Aurora; so Courtney, my daughter-in-law who speaks Spanish, and I drove up there with intentions of walking a Hispanic neighborhood with my petition. At the Republican headquarters a guy named Bill gave us a map and a route and said it was a "really great neighborhood with super nice people". After eight houses of no one being home we met Fran Shaw, a Republican precinct chair who was also walking the neighborhood with petitions, but she had, to her advantage, a map of Republican voters' addresses. Apparently, the demographics of the neighborhood we were in had changed over the years and was now predominantly Democrat and not Hispanic. Fran asked who I was walking for and I said…myself!

She proceeded to take us around to the homes of people she was sure would be happy to sign my petition. Knocking on doors, I met a couple who had just spoken to another Senate candidate, John Arrington, while at a soccer game. We talked for awhile and the husband said he would check out my website. We also met a very nice family with six children and expecting their seventh. The wife spoke with Fran and Courtney while the husband asked me several questions. He declared that "I passed" and he would remember me when he went to vote. Door to door campaigning is not the most efficient way to gain state-wide recognition, but the few hours we spent in Aurora reaped one great benefit—Fran. I had only a few volunteers helping me get my name and message out in Chicago and its collar counties and Fran became someone who showed continued support, keeping me posted on events taking place in Chicago, and distributing yard signs. I am particularly grateful for her willingness to speak in my behalf at events I was unable to attend.

My campaign manager forced me out of the house many times when I just didn't want to leave. She insisted that I go to Chicago, which was, at the start, my least favorite place; but after repeated trips to the city I grew to enjoy it. When my sisters came to visit in January (each lives out of state and each came for ten days) our trips to Chicago were actually fun. It takes more than three hours to drive from Springfield to Chicago and it was always easier and less stressful to have someone with me. Laura and I had been stretched to the limit during November and December trying to do everything that a staff of five or six would normally do. She was scheduling my events, keeping up with Facebook, ordering campaign materials, and taking care of all the administrative duties. I was learning the issues, answering questionnaires, and traveling, many times having to drive myself. When my sisters were here they did the driving and whatever event we attended they worked the crowd, passing out my literature, answering questions, making sure I had everything I needed, etc. After being in a sort of hell, this felt like heaven.

I never paid a driver, so either I drove myself or enlisted a volunteer to ride with me. My son, his wife, my campaign manager, my husband, my sisters, and a couple of volunteers took turns being my companion on my many trips around the state. Don Lowery almost always drove himself too. Patrick Hughes seemed to enjoy having the accoutrements of the campaign, and Becky and I always got a kick out of watching him pull up to events, a young driver behind the wheel. Mark Kirk had so many drivers I couldn't keep track of them. He also had lots of people to stand in for him at the events he couldn't (or wouldn't) attend. John Arrington had a driver. I'm not sure about Andy Martin…he just always seemed to appear out of nowhere.

In retrospect, it is clear that in order to adequately cover Illinois' fifty-eight thousand square miles and reach a good number of its eight point three million voters (of which only one point six million voted in the February 2010 Primary), I needed a much larger organization. Technology, of course, gave us an inexpensive and fast way to reach many people at one time, but every effort to get name recognition requires resources. I recently heard Sean Hannity suggest to his radio listeners that if they feel frustrated or anxious over the state of the country, then maybe they should get behind a candidate—volunteer a few hours or, if they don't have the extra time, donate a few dollars. It is so true that the two things a candidate needs to win are time and money.

Money

Does she have any idea how much this is going to cost?

On the evening of August nineteenth, 2009, while collecting signatures in the tent at the State Fair, John Parrot, treasurer for the Illinois Republican County Chairmen's Association, called. He let me know that I was invited, along with all of the other candidates, to speak to the Republican Party County Chairmen the following morning. He explained the order of events for the meeting and then, to my surprise, asked me if I would be willing, "for the sake of the Party and for the conservative values", to narrow the field to one conservative. I responded, "Absolutely, as long as that conservative is me!" He laughed a surprised kind of laugh and then asked me the exact same question again. When I gave the exact same answer, he asked if I would be able to raise one and one-half million dollars in two weeks because that, he said, is what I would need. I said, "I doubt it."

The tornado sirens began to blare, so I hung up and headed for the safety of a brick exhibit building. The storm inside me equaled the one raging outside. I was fuming and upset. I called my niece, Hayden, an experienced campaigner who was working on her master's degree in political science. "No one can raise that kind of money in that short time!" she reassured me. John was simply trying to coax me out of the race—the first of several attempts by a variety of people.

About a week later it became perfectly clear to me that money does a lot of talking when you are running for office. At the State Fair in DuQuoin, Mark Kirk was the first to take the microphone on Republican Day. He showed the crowd a map of Illinois with lines drawn to all the places he had been. Maybe he thought this would impress us, but if we weren't he was sure we would be awed by the amount of money he had raised. With the Primary a full five months away he had one point six *million* dollars sitting in the bank. He never mentioned an issue and never told us why he would make us proud as our U.S. Senator. He just showed us his bank balance then bounced off the stage because he had "somewhere else to be". Another flag for his map, I suppose. There was no doubt the Party wanted the man with the money and I was becoming more determined to stay in the race.

I fielded a few questions. They were lobbed pretty softly and then the young man said, "How do you plan on raising 5 to 10 million before the primary?" I almost laughed because it was an asinine question. But I restrained myself and said, "Well, first of all, that amount is unrealistic. I plan on raising a modest sum and running on the issues."

Journal Entry-October 27

A Sangamon County Precinct Chairman, Bob Green, reported to me that Rosie Long from the Sangamon County

Republican headquarters had asked him, "Does she have any idea how much money this is going to cost?" Honestly, no, I hadn't a clue. In fact, on September 25th Laura and I went to Sam's Club to buy five hundred stamps which totaled $220. In my journal that night I wrote, "I think I'm reaching my financial limit!" Up to that point I had spent four thousand dollars of my own money. But each week during the campaign I found myself becoming more and more committed to offering Illinoisans something truly different. I would work diligently to retain our basic freedoms by returning to our Constitutional and Free Market roots. So each week I made a greater financial commitment. Dwight and I had been saving for a Christmas trip to Hawaii. When I decided to run, we postponed the vacation a year and in October I began dipping into the Hawaii fund. By November I realized that after the election we would have to begin saving all over again. Dwight started drawing Social Security in September and we began using that money for the campaign. In the end I spent twenty thousand dollars of our own money. For a middle class person, without deep pockets, this was no small amount.

Every person representing the Party asked me first, before they knew anything about me, "How much money do you have?" and "How do you plan on raising money?" Every Tea Party member, 9/12er and unattached voter (with one exception) wanted to know my stand on the issues—Cap and Trade, abortion, gun control, and healthcare being of most concern. Kirk didn't need to address the issues because he could spend his way to a Primary victory. Besides, drawing attention to his liberal voting record would not have been to his advantage when talking to conservative voters.

I remember calling a Republican County Chairman in one of the Chicago suburbs and asking him how much literature I could send him for distribution. His first question for me was "How do you expect to raise money if you win?" He didn't even ask if I was a conservative or moderate or anything about my stand on policy—only the money mattered to him. This is one way the Republican Party is failing us. The message they send to voters is that money comes first—before character, intelligence, ability, and political ideology. This backwards thinking is one reason we have a Congress full of less than desirables.

> *They just announced on the radio that Mark Kirk has raised 1.6 million dollars to run in the Primary against some "lesser known candidates." Yes, that would be me.*
>
> *Journal Entry-October 5*

Asking people for money is difficult for me because I understand how hard they work for it. One day at the State Fair a complete stranger pulled out forty dollars, offering it as a donation for the campaign. I refused it, in part, because I felt awkward taking his money, but also because we were not equipped for accepting money. We had yet to set up a bank account and were still learning the rules for donations. Every dollar needed to be accounted for and Federal rules say that campaigns must make "best effort" to obtain the name, address, occupation and employer for every donor. We studied the literature of more experienced politicians and Laura designed a donation form for people to fill out when making contributions. Most importantly, I had to do two things right away: one, file with the Federal Elections Commission and, two, find someone willing to be my campaign treasurer.

I called the man who had been Treasurer for the school board on which I had served. He was a CPA and I knew he would be a great campaign treasurer. I also knew that with his business, his volunteer work for the school board, and as his son's soccer coach, he would probably not have time for this responsibility. I was right in that, but he did give me the name of a recently retired CPA who he thought would be a perfect match; his name was Gerald Aldrich. I called Gerry and he said that he had been praying for an opportunity to become politically active and he felt that I was an answer to his prayers. I told him that, likewise, he was an answer to our prayers! Laura and I, aside from knowing how to live within a budget, and believing that people (and the government) should not spend more than they have, were pretty much bookkeeping idiots. It was a total relief to be able to turn over the entire financial operation to Gerry. He and I were not a one hundred percent political ideological match, but we were close enough and more importantly, I sensed he had integrity and I instantly trusted him. He kept track of every penny during the campaign and made sure we were on time when filing with the Federal Elections Commission.

Nearly everything in a campaign costs money—paper, envelopes, stamps, signs, business cards, brochures, photocopying, ads, gas, etc. Being new to campaigning, we had to research and weigh every decision that involved spending money. Every mailing was done carefully—we had to make sure each letter, envelope, and stamp would reap positive returns in the way of votes. Email played a critical role in our campaign efforts. It was the fastest and most efficient way to contact groups of people at one time. Laura and LB kept a growing list of email addresses which they used to get out campaign updates and fundraising letters. In our mass electronic mailings we would ask the recipient to forward our message on to people on their email lists. We used Facebook to communicate with supporters and tried our hand at Twitter, both free venues for social networking. The cost of getting my website up and running was well worth the money as the site proved important to information seekers.

My friends and relatives were very generous with monetary contributions. Friends from Texas who I had not seen for decades gave generously when they heard I was running. Complete strangers who had either heard me speak, read about me, or searched my website made on-line donations. Every penny was needed and appreciated and we were careful with how we used the money. In a campaign update sent out via email and dated January 6th, I stated:

*I am repeatedly asked by Party leaders about my campaign finances. My answer to them is this—we are in economic difficult times. The actions of Congress are making our economic future unsure. People are worried about their jobs, their businesses and the fast-rising cost of living. For this reason I am not aggressively seeking campaign contributions to finance this Primary race. It would be unconscionable for me to do so. I am very grateful for those of you who show your support for me with your money and time. We are running an effective frugal campaign and **I promise to continue to treat your tax dollars with the same respect and frugality after I am elected your Senator.***

Note: A December poll reported in the Chicago Tribune had Kathleen Thomas tied with Hughes, who spent more than 10 times what she did. Substance can matter.

"Pay to play" presented its ugly self in various forms on the campaign trail. Disregard by Party leaders was frustrating, but it was not the only way a money-poor candidate like me was shunned. There were plenty of events I was invited to, but did not attend because they were cost prohibitive. For example, I received invitations to power dinners sponsored by various Republican organizations which cost fifty to hundreds of dollars per plate. Incentives to pay for the dinners included the opportunity to speak and mingle with the rich and powerful in the Party. "Sponsorships" were usually available which meant you could pay for an entire table for a thousand dollars or so and bring people to fill the table. Other than Mark Kirk, Patrick Hughes was the only Republican Primary Senate candidate that I know of who participated in any of this. I appreciated so much the chili dinners, soup and sandwich suppers, barbeques, and buffet breakfasts sponsored by many of the Republican organizations throughout the state These events generally drew a good number of informed and interested people and I was more than happy to pay the ten, fifteen, or even twenty dollars to attend and often address the group. I thought that spending exorbitant amounts of money on a Primary campaign was obscene. Don Lower had written a powerful press release chastising the Party for the practice of pay-to-play.

I had decided early that I would spend the bulk of my money on radio ads during the month of January. When I called around to inquire about the cost, I was delighted to learn that they had a special "campaign" rate that started about six weeks out from the Primary. Of course Kirk's campaign knew all of this already (when you've been in Congress for five terms, you pretty much have the election process down) and had everything in place while we scrambled just to keep our heads above water. In November, we started getting "political rate cards" which broke down the cost of advertising by length of the ad, the time of day it airs and, in some cases, the part of the state in which it would be aired—Chicago air time was about six times more expensive than the same time downstate.

Metro Traffic and News out of Chicago sent us one of the first rate cards we received. We decided to go with them because of the wide range of stations and listeners they had. So, on December 2nd, after a television interview, Courtney and I stopped at Metro Traffic to record four 10-15 second ads, which would be aired as sponsorships of traffic and news reports throughout the state. It sounded like a perfect plan and we said this was what we wanted to do, so they worked up a fee schedule and showed it to Laura and me at a later meeting. We tried not to let the shock show on our faces when we saw the $25,620 price tag. Apparently the salesman had misunderstood me when I said we were operating on a *small* budget.

They continued to work with us and soon delivered an excellent package that we could afford. We were pleased with the product they delivered. Leading up to my ad a DJ would say something like, "The news (or traffic report) is brought to you by Kathleen Thomas for U.S. Senate" then this or another ad would play:

I'm Kathleen Thomas and I approve this message. Illinois is known for corruption and dirty politics. We are better than that. Do something different and vote for Kathleen Thomas. Learn more at KathleenThomasForSenate.com.

Then a recorded announcer's voice would say, *"Paid for by Friends of Kathleen Thomas for Senate."* All in all, my name was said five times during the ten second sponsorship. Later I recorded full sixty second ads in Springfield which were aired throughout the state. I believe that many of the votes I received, from the Chicago area especially, were due to these radio spots. Of the $30,000 campaign budget, about $10,000 was spent on radio ads. With our limited coffers, we felt the ads were money well spent.

While more money would definitely have been an asset, I believe there should be limits set on the money spent in a primary election. Of the $2,241,467 spent on the Republican Senate Primary in Illinois, 75% of that was spent by Mark Kirk. The other five candidates spent the rest, or 25%. Of the 742,266 total Republican votes cast, Mark Kirk received 56.6%. The other five candidates together received 43.4%. There seems to have been a disproportionate amount of money spent for the number of votes received. Maybe setting a cap on how much can be spent during a *Primary* would help level the playing field. A glance at the cost per vote for each candidate seems to confirm this.

Money Spent per Vote

Patrick Hughes	$4.56
Mark Kirk	4.02
John Arrington	1.64
Donald Lowery	.59
Kathleen Thomas	.57
Andy Martin	(No financial activity reported)

Polls

...we celebrated our second place in the poll.

Members of the political culture can't wait to get their fingers on the voter's collective pulse. The first day to file with the State Board of Elections was October 26, but we were aware of polls being conducted weeks before this date. Fortunately, we were unaware of the polls that had been done months before I even decided to run. In fact, many candidates conducted their own polls as part the "testing of the waters" process. Jim Ryan paid for such a poll "to underscore his strength among Illinois voters" in the Gubernatorial race. The results had him 22 percentage points ahead of the next candidate and practically discounted Kirk Dillard as a formidable rival. (Illinois Review, Oct. 6, 2009) In the Primary election, a different candidate, Bill Brady, received 150 more votes than Dillard to win the gubernatorial nomination for the Republican Party...Ryan's poll may have merely given Ryan the confidence to jump in the race.

In October, we stumbled across an online poll conducted by the Illinois Review. They asked, "If the Primary were held today, who would you vote for U.S. Senate?" The poll was up for several days. Kathleen Thomas supporters voted; we suspect some more than once. There were so few participants that every time one person voted the percentage points jumped up. At campaign headquarters we dismissed the poll as anything important and were certain readers saw through it. In fact, Laura wrote in an email to one volunteer:

The poll was only open for 24 hours and not many people saw it. We did get Kathy up from 1.6 to 13.4% before it ended. The leading candidate (and the one with the most money) only got 34%. If nothing else, it was fun to watch the numbers rise. I doubt anyone puts any stock in that sort of poll. (October 6, 2009)

The results were posted the following day in an article with very serious overtones. Readers' comments on the article and poll were equally as serious and some were obviously made by members of one camp or another.

Because *some* polls are legitimate, people tend to give credence to *all* polls. Some polls are more reliable than others, but a person is apt to pay attention to all poll results, even those that are manipulated or not legitimate. This works to the advantage of the candidate who commissions his own polls to promote himself. Undoubtedly, thinking people realized that Jim Ryan's poll, indicating that 33% of people viewed him favorably over the other gubernatorial candidates who barely rose above single digits, was an inflated view of reality. But because his numbers were so incredibly high, one couldn't help but believe that he was a viable candidate. Campaigns conduct these initial polls presumably to help them decide whether the candidate should bother running or not. But interestingly, polls serve other important functions. They can (1) convince the public that their candidate stands a chance at winning and (2) provide the public with more "good news" about the candidate, thus building favorable image. It becomes a cycle that feeds on itself.

There were only two legitimate polls done for the U.S. Senate race before the Primary. This was understandable, considering the huge lead in popularity and money Mark Kirk had. Both polls were conducted by the Chicago Tribune. Here is the breakdown of the poll taken in mid-December:

```
Kirk...............................
41%
Thomas..............................
3%
Hughes..............................
.3%
Arrington...........................
2%
Martin..............................
...2%
Lowery..............................
.1%
Other...............................
..1%
Undecided...........................
46%
```

As ri... ...ed our 2nd place in the p... campaign off the intere... s spending money like h... eon for the gubernatorial ...y used the poll to my ad... and gave my usual shtick and then I mentioned that I was second in the poll. I did not, of course, mention that I was tied with Patrick or how far down from first place I was. People were impressed.

More than anything, a poll of this kind gives you an idea of whose name is most recognizable. The interesting fact in this poll, however, was that 76% of the Primary voters polled

Apologies... *we are sorry about the printing error on page 92. Below is the chart and the paragraph covered up by it.*

Kirk	41%
Thomas	3%
Hughes	3%
Arrington	2%
Marrin	2%
Lowery	1%
Other	1%

As ridiculous as it may sound, we celebrated our 2nd place in the poll. After all, Mark Kirk could run his campaign off the interest of his millions and Patrick Hughes was spending money like he was Mark Kirk. At a December luncheon for the gubernatorial candidates in Bloomington, I delightedly used the poll to my advantage. I talked about the Constitution and gave my usual shtick and then I mentioned that I was second in the poll. I did not, of course, mention that I was tied with Patrick or how far down from first place I was. People were impressed.

considered themselves conservative. If we total the percentages for the conservative candidates (Thomas, Hughes, Arrington, Martin, Lowery, and other) and throw all the undecided voters into the mix, we are only at 58%. So, *at least* 18% of the conservative voters were choosing the liberal voting Mark Kirk. As the campaign wore on, I realized that there was a huge number of Kirk supporters who had no clue how liberal the Congressman's record was.

Patrick Hughes commissioned several polls during the fall months. In at least one, the pollster asked who was favored, Hughes or Kirk. (The other four candidates were not mentioned). Those people who said "Kirk" would then be told about his liberal voting record and Hughes' conservative platform and then asked again who they would vote for. The numbers jumped considerably in Hughes' favor when the voter was informed. Many people argued that this was not a true or fair poll, and I agree. Nonetheless, it was an interesting comment on the *type* of candidate people really wanted— conservative. The polls conducted by Hughes were generally no more than gimmicks to grow support for him.

At the end of October, four days before filing my petitions, I called the Concerned Citizens of America (CCA) organization that was hosting a candidates' forum in Rockford. We had read the announcement in a Winnebago County GOP e-newsletter.

The event was set for the 26th—the same day I would file and more than three months before the Primary. I told the woman I was speaking with on the phone that I was trying to adjust my schedule because I really wanted to attend their forum.

"How much time would I have to speak?" I asked. She said, all in one breath, "Oh yes, I was going to talk to you because the GOP had forwarded that email to you by mistake and I was going to talk to you about this and we really have a schedule and there are certain people coming and it really was sent by mistake and…" I interrupted and said, "So, what you're saying is that I'm not invited."

"Well, yes, that would be correct." And I said, "Well, I'm certainly glad I called." To which she responded, "Oh, I was going to call you."

CANDIDATE FORUMS -- Who are the real conservatives?
Conservative candidates need your votes in the Primary in order to become the conservative candidate in the November General Election…these forums will help you make this informed decision!

Monday, October 26th: SENATORIAL CANDIDATE FORUM CCA
Monday, November 2nd: GUBERNATORIAL CANDIDATE FORUM

Both events are at Stockholm Inn (Rockford, IL) at 6:30 pm.
Complimentary dessert. Donations accepted. RSVP to XXXXXX (phone #); seating is limited. Straw polls will be taken of those in attendance; come and make your opinion count!

"So, tell me, who are the candidates invited."

"Well, Mark Kirk, Patrick Hughes, Eric Wallace, Arrington, and oh, who is it? His name escapes me, who is it? (nervous laughter)."

"Zadek?" I asked.

"Yes, that's it, Zadek."

"Oh, I see. The five men from Chicago."

"I'm so sorry, I hope you understand. But there are so many candidates and if we invited them all we would be here for several hours."

"Oh, no, I understand. I understand perfectly."

They were trying to squeeze Don Lowery and myself out of the race to keep us from getting a footing at the start. They didn't take me seriously and they grossly underestimated my determination and grit. I was not going away.

It was at this event that the first straw poll for the race took place. Don Lowery didn't bother to find out if he had been invited or not (a far better approach than mine) and just showed up. He later informed me as to what transpired that evening.

The Illinois Right of Way Daily Blog, which describes itself as an "uncensored free-for-all where anyone can post – regardless of age or style", published a press release from Patrick Hughes' campaign.

U. S. SENATE CANDIDATE PATRICK HUGHES WINS CONCERNED CITIZENS FOR AMERICA PAC STRAW POLL

Concerned Citizens for America PAC held a candidates forum on Monday in Rockford and has just released the results of its straw poll in the GOP race for U.S. Senate in Illinois. U.S. Senate candidate Patrick Hughes has won the straw poll with an overwhelming 45% of the vote, more than the combined totals of his two closest competitors who participated in the forum and straw poll.

"I am very pleased to have won the straw poll and anticipate, with great enthusiasm, the official endorsement of Concerned Citizens for America PAC," said Patrick Hughes. "It is wonderful to know that our message of mainstream Republican values is getting out and is being so well-received

Of course Hughes won the straw poll! According to Lowery, whether Hughes knew it or not, the forum was created for that purpose. They knew Mark Kirk would not show and they limited the number of candidates invited in order to inflate the numbers. About eighty people attended. Patrick Hughes was there with his entourage and supporters. Everyone voted. Patrick gets to brag about winning the straw poll and then publicly suggests that he could very well be endorsed by the CCA PAC.

Election Day

Thank you for the opportunity to have a vote that meant something to me.

fter the pressures of the previous six months, the activities of February 1st were like light housework. Loretta and I answered emails and phone calls, we washed the car and checked out the yard signs that were up around town—adding some where there weren't any and fixing those that had fallen down. We stopped at a VFW to see if anything was going on there. Inside we found just one lady who explained she could not exhibit my literature because it was a polling place, but she took my card. I took Loretta to the airport to catch her flight home and gave my card to the woman at the rental car desk. After a brief discussion, she said she would be sure to vote for me. Then I drove downtown to the Presidential Library to see a friend and made a few phone calls while I sat in my parked car. I

Voting day!

Journal Entry-Feb

inadvertently left my keys turned in the ignition and ended up with a dead battery. Dwight came to give the car a jump then I went home to answer more emails. I called Laura and we both realized that there was nothing more we could do. It was all so anticlimactic. Tomorrow was Election Day.

Dwight and I got up early on February 2nd and voted at the Knights of Columbus. It was pure pleasure to walk into the voting booth and vote for a true conservative *and* a woman. That moment alone made all of the thousands of stressful and discouraging moments dissolve into the satisfaction of having done what the political pundits had been suggesting. Do something…and I *had* done something…different.

We returned home and walked the dog to the yard sign that was posted at the entrance to our subdivision. We stood there and waved at a few cars…it was bitterly cold and I was simultaneously exhausted and exhilarated. Back at home I talked on the phone to several voters making their last minute voting decisions and answered their questions about my view of the issues. By the end of each call, the voter had said he or she would vote for me. Laura came over for awhile and we discussed the fact that we felt we had done everything we could. We had given it our best shot and we decided we had stretched our monetary and time resources to their absolute limit. We had reaped the maximum results from what we had.

The results of the election confirmed this. Mark Kirk spent 50 times the amount of money as I did and received 7.7 times the number of votes. Patrick Hughes spent over 16 times the amount that I did and garnered 2.6 times the number of votes.

The 2010 election cycle began early in Illinois—in 2008 the state Democrats had pushed the Primary from March to the first week in February in order to draw greater national attention to Presidential candidate, Barrack Obama. This was unfortunate for several reasons, the first being practical. In addition to the fact that the campaigning period was shortened, the Thanksgiving and Christmas holiday seasons forced us to be put on hold for a week or two. Also, the typically bad Illinois weather in January made travel difficult. In some incidents, snow and ice forced forums to cancel, and attendance at some events was lower than expected. I would not let the weather and road conditions stop me from attending an event, but all of my travelling companions refused to go with me when the forecast called for ice or heavy snow. I was ready to chance the icy roads one morning after a bad storm when Randy White called to let me know that the Peoria events had been cancelled. Worried about the danger the roads posed, he took it upon himself to let the other candidates know about the cancellation. January 2010 was extremely cold; the ground was frozen so solid that it was nearly impossible to get the yard signs posted. The worst of it was that an early winter Primary meant that candidates and voters had less time and opportunity to become acquainted.

Most people don't pay attention to campaign efforts until a few weeks before Election Day; everything I did before January was laying the groundwork for those last weeks. There was no campaigning the week between Christmas and New Year's Day, so I spent that time studying the issues and trying to rest and do "normal" things—spending time with the grandkids, going to movies with Dwight (*Avatar, Sherlock Holmes* and *Invictus* all in four days time), walking the dog, and cleaning our neglected house. I remember waking up on December 30th with a sore throat and thinking, "…not good, not good at all. I cannot get sick at this point." My calendar was full for the month of January right up until the February 2nd Primary and I had to be at my best. Flu season is a terrible time for campaigning. My symptoms just kept getting worse, but I battled on for over a week giving interviews and speaking (barely) at my scheduled events. Fortunately, the two days I had no voice were also the same two days the weather was the worst, and all events were cancelled.

We seemed to be campaigning in the middle of a revival-like atmosphere. Even the inclement weather could not keep the most devoted of the electorate away from the forums I attended. The rumblings of discontented conservatives were beginning to be heard during the spring of 2009. On April 15th, "tea parties" were held across the nation, drawing attention to the fact that many Americans were unhappy with the direction our government was taking us. During that summer and fall, 9/12 and Tea Party groups were springing up across the country and Illinois was no exception.

The conservative movement was energized when Republican Scott Brown came from behind to win a U.S. Senate seat in traditionally liberal Massachusetts. Friends on my Facebook page were giving each other high fives. Although Brown was not one hundred percent conservative, his come-from-behind win in such a blue state gave hope to conservatives who wanted to make big changes in Washington. Columnist Jeffrey T. Kuhner wrote that Brown's victory "has provided conservatives with a golden opportunity to build a national majority coalition upon the wreckage of Mr. Obama's presidency. The more to the left Mr. Obama veers, the more intense is the popular backlash" (The Washington Times, February 1, 2010, p. 31).

The conservative mood was and is a reflection of my beliefs. I entered the Illinois' U.S. Senate race to offer myself as a 'citizen legislator' and to show that an average citizen can run for office. I was not a new convert to the Constitution. I had been carrying a pocket version of the Constitution, the

Declaration of Independence, and the Bill of Rights in my purse since 2000. One of the statements on my campaign literature was to say "NO" to government that oversteps its authority and ignores the Constitution. So, the conservative movement building across the country was an easy fit for me and I did not have to "adjust" my political philosophy to become a conservative candidate...I was and am-conservative.

To the amazement of some, I became politically astute without a staff, without years of experience inside the beltway, and without Party support. What I lacked were two crucial ingredients—money and a statewide organization. I believe there are people in the state of Illinois who not only have a conservative philosophy, an agreeable personality, and integrity, but also have the money and the organization. As concerned Americans we need to encourage those people to run for office and then work to get them elected.

A key to improving the election process is to level the playing field. In our present system incumbents have the greater advantage in an election. In fact, over ninety percent of the time, incumbents are re-elected because they have access to money and other resources—not because they have done a particularly good job in office. Another key is in educating the electorate. In an ideal world, the electorate would study each candidate and make a determination on the information they had gathered. They wouldn't rely on the Party or some organization to tell them how to vote.

A few days before the election, I had attended an event sponsored by Adam Andrzejewski (a gubernatorial candidate who had been endorsed by Rush Limbaugh). During the course of Adam's speech, he mentioned that the state of Illinois needed a drastic change, something truly different. Then he said, "I will be okay with whatever the people decide at the polls. Maybe they're not ready for someone as outside of the mainstream as I am." Personally, this proved to be a profound statement, as I also had attempted to offer the people of Illinois something different. I realize that my expectations of the electorate were unrealistic; I assumed voters would thoroughly research every candidate and then make an educated decision when they cast their votes.

I believe, however, that the current political atmosphere of discontent will force the American people to undergo an educational process, which may include some hardship, before we are awakened to the fact that our government is drastically straying from our constitutional principles.

As the Primary drew close, we were asked by a number of newspapers and television stations where I would be on election night. I had originally planned on staying home to watch the results with Dwight, but Laura Gough decided to host an open house. It was a low-key event where people brought food and several computers were placed throughout the house so we could conveniently view the outcome. It was clear early in the evening that Kirk was the winner of the Senate race. Surprisingly, even to myself, I was *not* upset, bewildered, baffled, or stumped by this. Drawing on my faith in God, I had prayed and fasted to be able to emotionally handle whatever happened. After the grueling previous six months, I knew I would need sustaining support from a power greater than my own.

The day after the election, en route to St. Louis, I had a post-election interview over the phone with a newspaper journalist. When the interviewer asked how I was feeling after having lost the nomination, I responded with, "fine". She seemed confused by the idea that I was really *okay* with the election results, and so she asked again how I was doing. I said, "No, really, I am quite content with what I accomplished. I stepped up to the plate and as difficult as it turned out to be, I stood my ground and offered myself to the people of Illinois. I did it with a minimal amount of money and resources and no prior political experience." I also told her that I had a good life outside of the political realm. I had my faith, children, grandchildren, interests, a job—many things to keep me grounded.

During this interview I shared what I thought served as a good analogy of what I discovered during my bid for the United Stated Senate. In the *Lord of the Rings* trilogy some characters come under the spell of the ring, or "precious" as it is referred to. They are literally consumed with the desire to possess the ring and will sacrifice anything and anyone to obtain the ring. Likewise, some candidates were under the spell of the opportunity for power and money (a certain amount of notoriety and $172,000 plus perks were nothing to sneeze at). I noticed how some candidates would change their stance on certain issues, cater to the crowd, or say things that just weren't true. They were driven by the desire for that power.

Epilogue

I fear it is all about the money.

Six months of madness had come to an end and I was not exactly the same person I had been when it started. Had I known before I began this journey—how difficult, stressful and anxiety-filled it would be—I never would have attempted it. It is a good thing we cannot see into the future, otherwise, we would never take risks. I am extremely grateful I had this opportunity to offer the voters of Illinois something different. I had the smarts, eventually gained the confidence, but the money was always an issue. Every dollar donated, especially from people I didn't even know, garnered my appreciation and increased my humility. These supporters were honest, hard-working, thoughtful people who had done their homework. I was sincere in presenting myself and what I believed in, and I think people sensed that I said what I meant and meant what I said, and that they could vote for me with confidence.

On February second the people of Illinois had six candidates to choose from in the Republican Senate Primary— John Arrington, Patrick Hughes, Mark Kirk, Don Lowery, Andy Martin, and me. The majority of voters chose Mark Kirk. As I see it, people voted for Mark Kirk for one of three reasons: 1) The electorate was liberal and wanted someone who voted Yes for Cap and Trade, No to ban partial birth abortion, and did not mind his grade of F from the NRA, or 2) The electorate wanted a conservative Republican, but rather than voting for one of the conservative choices, they felt that Kirk had the money and organization to win, they hoped he would begin voting more conservatively, and they just held their noses and voted for him, or 3) The electorate were totally ignorant of Kirk's record and voted as the Party seemed to dictate. Now, I can live with number one, this is a Republic, after all, and the majority get who they want; but it is numbers two and three with which I have issues. I believe we have held our noses too many times when we vote, making our government mediocre at best. We need to work harder at getting candidates acceptable to a majority of people…candidates with integrity, if nothing else. The citizenry of this country can no longer afford to remain ignorant. We have to keep ourselves informed no matter how much trouble or how much time it takes. Being involved in government and politics needs to be a greater priority for all of us.

I am sure that to Kirk and his staff, the rest of the Senate candidates amounted to nothing more than mere bothersome gnats. But to over 320,000 voters, we were the voting option with greater appeal because either we reflected their conservative views or we offered them that "something different" they desired in their Senator.

From the first day I stepped into the tent at the State Fair until near Election Day, there was talk that having so many conservatives on the ballot would split the vote, ensuring a Kirk victory. The total final conservative vote count was still 100,000 less than the total votes Kirk received. So, in one sense, it would not have mattered if there was only one conservative running against the liberal—the liberal Kirk, with the millions of dollars and Party support, would still have won. But what if we had all rallied around Patrick Hughes, as Patrick had encouraged us to do? Would enough Kirk supporters have jumped ship and backed him? I doubt it. In my opinion, Hughes was lacking in too many areas to have garnered significant additional votes.

I fear it is all about the money. After the election, I received a call from Mark Kirk. He left a message on my voice mail thanking me for participating in the process and for caring about country and God. I also received a call from Curt Conrad, Illinois Executive Director for the Republican Party. He mentioned that, in the past, the Party had not done a good job of reaching out to losing participants in Republican Primary races. He wanted to keep the lines of communication open. I said I would love to talk with him, and as soon as I returned from an extended time away to see a new grandbaby and my parents, I would come in and visit.

Toward the end of March I stopped by Republican Headquarters in Springfield. I met Curt walking down the hall and we chatted for awhile. I was surprised he never invited me into his office to sit and talk. I was also surprised that he didn't ask if I would be willing to work for or if I would support Mark Kirk in any way.

After a few pleasantries were exchanged, I asked if he knew of anyone that was running as an Independent. He responded "Not yet, but if anyone does I will do everything in my power to make sure they don't get on the ballot. My job now is to promote and protect my candidates."

"Why do you think the Republican Party jumped out there so quickly to support Mark Kirk?" I asked.

"What do you mean?"

"Well, they were promoting him long before we were gathering signatures in August."

"Now, the Party never supported him. They never came out and said they were supporting him. The NRSC [National Republican Senatorial Committee] did support him early on."

"I just know that Michael Steele (President of the Republican National Committee) said the Party shouldn't get involved in Primaries."

"Yes, but he endorsed Mark Kirk also."

I stated that the quarter million plus votes that Hughes, Lowery, and I got were no small amount. He agreed that that was a big chunk of votes. When I asked him if he thought these votes would swing over to Kirk he said yes, the voters in Primaries were hard core Party people and they would vote for Kirk, who was going to be seeking after the Independent voter. When I mentioned the Tea Party groups and the 9/12ers, Conrad stated that he hoped they would not form a 3rd party. I said that according to everyone I had talked with and everything I had seen, there was not a desire to form a third party but rather a desire to have the Republican Party return to its conservative roots. He also mentioned that this was the most diverse ticket the (Illinois) Republicans had ever had…a Hispanic, an Asian, a downstater, and a woman (the token Judy Baar Topinka.) The Hispanic and Asian had run unopposed in the Primary and I found it interesting that a person living downstate would be termed a "diverse" candidate. Conrad said that State Senator Brady, (the conservative downstater that squeaked out the

Gubernatorial nomination), "needs to spend every day of the campaign in Chicago!" He added that Illinois politics were more different than anywhere else—except Louisiana.

His parting remark in reference to Kirk was *not*... "I've never seen a better candidate, I've never seen a more moderate candidate that can hold the party together, I've never seen a candidate work a crowd better than he does, I've never seen a candidate that can be a conservative at one meeting and a moderate at another as well as he does"... *no*, his parting words were... *"I've never seen a better fund raiser than Mark Kirk. He is amazing. He can pick up the phone and in a couple of weeks have several million dollars!"* I was neither surprised nor insulted that he reiterated the same song I had heard from so many Party Chair people who had stated the criteria they were looking for was money and name recognition. I am convinced, now more than ever before, that the Republican Party needs to return to being the Party of ideas and principles, and that the Party is a means to an end, not an end in itself.

I hope that my experience and submersion in the election process has benefited more than just me. I hope I have helped people see through political strategies such as polling and endorsements. I personally will never look at endorsements in the same way. I will never listen to what journalists write about politicians in the same light as I used to; and I will never take political ads at face value. Sadly, I learned that money talks (really loudly!) and I will never take for granted the funding of political campaigns. Lastly, I hope, for the sake of our country, that good people all over these United States will consider running for office. And I hope the electorate will look beyond image and beyond party and vote for people with honesty and integrity.

Fifty years ago, in response to Medicaid, Richard Weaver, a Chicago University professor and one of the founders of conservatism said, "The past shows unvaryingly that when a people's freedom disappears, it goes not with a bang, but in silence amid the comfort of being cared for. That is the dire peril in the present trend toward statism." The only way we can keep our freedom is to work at it. Not some of us--all of us. Not some of the time, but all of the time. If we value our citizenship and want to keep it for ourselves and our children and their children, we must be active in civic affairs. I hope that the electorate take to heart the reality that good candidates will not be elected to office and lead our country without money and organization, and in these two areas everyone can make a difference.

Addendum 1

February 2nd, 2010 Illinois U.S. Senate Primary Results

<u>Republican Primary</u>

Kirk   419,149   56.6%

Hughes   142,522   19.3%

Lowery   66,173   8.9%

Thomas   53,914   7.3%

Martin   37,359   5.0%

Arrington   21,016   2.8%

<u>Democratic Primary</u>

Giannoulias   351,120   38.9%

Hoffman   303,719   33.7%

Jackson   178,941   19.8%

Marshall   51,606   5.7%

Meister   16,232   1.8%

Addendum 2

Candidates as they appeared on the ballot:

Donald Lowery

Mark Kirk

Andy Martin

Kathleen Thomas

John Arrington

Patrick Hughes

Total disbursements Candidates Spent on Senate Campaign According to FEC (in order of expenditures)

Filing is for the period 1-1-09 to 1-13-10

Mark Kirk	$1,687,925
Patrick Hughes	651,392
John Arrington	34,640
Donald Lowery	38,942
Kathleen Thomas	30,874

Andy Martin (No financial activity reported)

ADDENDUM 3

Platform of the Illinois Republican Party

PREAMBLE

We, the Illinois Republican Party, since the election of 1860, the Republican Party has had a special calling – to advance the founding principles of freedom, opportunity, and limited government and the dignity and worth of every individual. Illinois Republicans have provided critical leadership, to this Country and those causes, from Abraham Lincoln to Ronald Reagan, from Everett M. Dirksen to Henry J. Hyde.

These principles form the foundation of both an agenda for America in the year 2008 and this Platform for our Party. They point us toward reforms in government, a restoration of timeless values, and a renewal of our national purpose.

We commit ourselves to the values that strengthen our culture and sustain our nation: family, faith, personal responsibility, and a belief in the dignity of every human life.

We offer not only an agenda but also a vision of a welcoming society in which all who yearn for freedom and human dignity have a place. To all law-abiding Americans, particularly immigrants and minorities, we send a clear message: this is the party of freedom and progress, and it is your home.

We are the party of the open door to those who share our principles, determined to strengthen the social, cultural, and political ties that bind us together and make our country the greatest force for good in the world. Steadfast in our commitment to our ideals, we recognize, as did Ronald Reagan, that members of our party can have deeply held and sometimes differing views. This diversity is a source of strength, not a sign of weakness, and so we welcome into our ranks all who may hold differing positions on issues but who will not compromise on our shared bedrock principles. We commit to resolve our differences with civility, trust, and mutual respect.

We seek to be faithful to the best traditions of our party. We are the party that ended slavery, protected life, granted homesteads, built land grant colleges, and moved control out of Washington, back into the hands of the people. We believe in service to the common good – and that good is not common until it is shared.

Our vision is one of clear direction, new ideas, civility in public life, and leadership with honor and distinction.

To the citizens of Illinois, we commit ourselves to the following:

- To conduct ourselves in such a way as to rebuild the public trust in the Republican Party and in government as institutions of public service and not personal gain;
- To do all in our power to strengthen the families of Illinois;
- To protect the fundamental right to life and dignity of every human life;
- To provide a foundation for job creation and business expansion across the State and reduce regulations and taxes that smother the free market;

- To enlist Illinois in defending America's borders;
- To endorse necessary resources and appropriate strategies to combat terrorist attacks and to fight and win the war on terror;
- To make our communities safer through reducing crime and drug use;
- To safeguard our way of life through adoption of sensible energy resource policies;
- To promote Illinois' advantage as a transportation hub for the nation;
- To create an environment in which our public schools will become the best in the nation;
- To reduce the size of government and the number of citizens dependent upon government;
- To ensure that high quality health care is available, through the private sector, throughout our State in both rural and urban areas;
- To restore fairness and balance to a legal system that has become unfair and unbalanced;
- To safeguard Illinois' fundamental crop – our agricultural sector; and
- To maintain our stewardship of our natural resources through scientifically sound and economically balanced initiatives.

OUR PARTY's PHILOSOPHY

The cornerstone of our democracy and of the Republican Party is found in the Declaration of Independence:

"We hold these truths to be self-evident: That all men are created equal; that they are endowed by their Creator with certain unalienable rights; that among these are life, liberty, and the pursuit of happiness." From these principles flow our commitment to Equality, Freedom, and The Right to Life, Opportunity, Less Government, Low Taxes and Strong National Security. The Republican Party is unwavering in its commitment to these principles.

We honor the Constitution and believe that neither the Executive, Legislative nor Judicial branches of government should detract from the rights enumerated therein.

*The complete platform can be found at:
http://www.weareillinois.org/learn/resources.aspx

ABOUT THE AUTHORS

Kathleen Smith Thomas lives in Springfield, Illinois, with her husband Dwight and dog Kipper. They have three children, and five geographically distant, but perfect grandchildren. She received her PhD in Humanities from Florida State University. Prior to running for the Senate, Kathleen worked at the Old State Capitol researching the people and places of Abraham Lincoln's era.

Laura Oleen Gough graduated from Brigham Young University and later earned a Masters of Education degree at the University of North Carolina-Greensboro. She is married to Jeff and is actively involved in the lives of their four amazing children. They have enjoyed living in the "Land of Lincoln" for the past eight years.